CUT OFF

CUT OFF

behind enemy lines in the Battle of the Bulge
with two small children, Ernest Hemingway,
and other assorted misanthropes

BILL DAVIDSON

STEIN AND DAY/*Publishers*/New York

To Muriel and Carol, and to young Davidson, who is nearly that age.

This is a true story. I reconstructed it from notes I made at the time, and from my memory. If there are minor errors of fact —involving dates, places, and such— blame the memory.

Bill Davidson

PART I
Tarfu

December 16-19, 1944

1

I hadn't pushed my jeep more than two miles over the icy road out of what was now the ghost town of Spa, Belgium, when the little girl told me, in German, that she had to go to the bathroom.

Not that I understood German that well, but she'd said something that sounded like "toilet." I can't say I was surprised; after all, though she was only six years old, she was a woman. The last time I had driven from Paris to what was then the quiet Ardennes front, some snotty public relations major had pulled rank on me and insisted that I take three lady war correspondents as passengers in the jeep, each of whom had made me stop the jeep every fifteen minutes—all the way from the Place de la Concorde to the city of Luxembourg.

So now, when the little girl indicated a desire to relieve herself, I took it as a matter of course; and suppressing my naturally cowardly desire to get the hell away from Spa as quickly as I could—the way the entire U.S. First Army head-quarters apparently had—I pulled over to the shoulder of the comparatively broad but now ominously deserted Spa-Theux road. The little girl tried to climb down the high side of the jeep by herself but couldn't. Finally I got out and went around to help her. I was twenty-three, unmarried, with no nieces or nephews, and totally untutored in the ways and problems of kids. Hence the slowness of my mind, already dulled by fear, to realize that it is difficult for a three-foot individual to make a three-foot jump into crusted ice and snow.

A few minutes before, I had been told that her name was Lisa.

As she scrambled off into the bushes, I looked at her neat Mary Jane-type shoes, black stockings, blue coat, and the pointy blue knitted cap that came down over her ears, and wondered if there was some item of engineering in kids' underwear which she would require assistance in undoing. But she went off into the bushes and apparently was managing all right.

While Lisa was rustling around in the omnipresent Ardennes fir trees, I stood beside the jeep and stared hopelessly at her brother, who had remained seated in the vehicle. He was Friedrich, seven years old by the estimates that had been given me. The name seemed too cumbersome for a kid his size, so I was calling him Freddie. He too was warmly dressed in an overcoat, black stockings, and pointy cap, but of course he wore short pants instead of a skirt. By the look of their clothing, someone, I figured, must have been giving these children some loving care. But by the look in their eyes, big brown ones with a cloud over them, the care could not have obliterated what had gone before.

Freddie's eye-cloud deepened as we heard a "whoosh" filter down through the thick cold mist above our heads. Only one plane made a noise like that, the jet Messerschmitt 262. Our side didn't have any jets in Europe. I hadn't heard the "whoosh" —nothing but the steady propeller roar of our P-47's and P-38's —since the first few days after I had had the misfortune to land on Omaha Beach in Normandy. To myself I said, "What the fuck is going on? Where the hell are *our* guys?" To Freddie I said, "Come on, kid, while we're waiting we might as well take a leak, too."

The boy didn't understand a word, but I helped him down from the jeep. Somehow, I expected little boys to be less fragile than little girls, and I was surprised to feel the ribs of his scrawny body beneath his clothes. "Christ, kids are little," I thought.

As Freddie went with me behind the jeep, he hungrily watched to make sure to do everything I did. When I opened my fly, he opened his fly. When I zipped up, he zipped up. When I yawned nervously, he yawned nervously.

We stood around for a while, stamping our feet in the snow to keep warm, and then I began to worry about what was taking the little girl so long. I heard a faint sob off in the bushes where she had gone. Summoning up all my intuition and the smattering of pidgin German I had acquired from being exposed to New York Yiddish and from a girl in a besieged apartment during the Battle of Aachen, I shouted in the direction of the bushes, "What's the matter, kid? *Haben zie nicht kin papeer tzu weipen der ass?*"

A faint *"nein"* came out of the bushes.

I was tempted to tell her to root around in the snow for leaves, like everyone else, but I sighed and went over to the jeep, in the back of which was what some of my contemporaries enviously referred to as "Davidson's Lootwagen." In it, I had stashed such items as a felt bedroll from Fortnum and Mason (it had belonged to a British officer who wouldn't be needing it any more), a gross of sulphur-colored German Army contraceptives, vintage wines and cognacs from Verdun, hotel soap and towels from the George V in Paris and the Dorchester in London, a Galéries Lafayette silk dressing gown for nights away from the front, and—rarest of all—two rolls of tissue-soft toilet paper brought back from an illegal trip across the border into neutral Switzerland.

I reluctantly tore off a few sheets of the toilet paper and gave them to Freddie to take into the woods to Lisa. She came back with him and looked up at me with an expression of what I took to be gratitude.

The ME-262's whooshed overhead again. The children, who

13

obviously had heard them before, in another time and another place, began to tremble. In the silence along the empty road, I clearly could pick up the crescendo of distant heavy artillery fire from three directions—what I took to be north, east, and south.

I hoisted the kids back up in the jeep and they huddled together in the canvas-upholstered seat next to mine. Lisa was between Freddie and me, and I could feel her shivering, even through the thickness of my lined trench coat. I was shivering too, but not from the cold. Never, in the combat zone, had I seen such a normally well-traveled road as the five miles between Spa and Theux without a single vehicle on it—especially in the middle of the afternoon. When I had come down the road in the opposite direction less than an hour before, there had at least been a few jeeps, command cars, and trucks heading over to N 15, the main highway to Liège. Now, nothing.

A few minutes later we were in Theux, an ancient stone village consisting of a few stores and a church, clustered around a square in which there was the inevitable World War I monument. Although all these village monuments referred, in their chipped-stone lettering, to *"nos enfants"* who had fallen in battle, many of the people in this part of Belgium were German-speaking and I often wondered if they had been inclined to change *enfants* to *Kinder* during the Nazi occupation so recently ended. It didn't occur to me that the occupation might be resumed at any minute. It apparently had, however, occurred to the inhabitants of Theux. The stores and houses all were shuttered; the people probably had either fled or were hiding expectantly in their cellars.

I pulled up in the courtyard of the church to get my jeep out of line-of-sight, at least, from the square. Lisa and Freddie were looking at me gravely, obviously expecting me to exhibit some sort of leadership. So I got out of the jeep and pounded on the locked oaken doors of the church. No one answered, though I caught a glimpse of a frightened white face peering at me through one of the semi-stained-glass windows.

I went back to the jeep and drove it further into the courtyard. Then I found my red-covered Michelin Atlas (no plain old military maps for me) and tried to make some geographical sense out of the red and yellow squiggles. With the biting cold mist, the temperature probably had dropped by now to about 30 degrees and I had to put on my gloves as I turned the pages of the atlas.

I heard Lisa crying softly just beside me. Despite all my *"vas is los's"* and other attempts at communication, neither she nor Freddie would tell me what was wrong. Finally I reached back into the jeep and hauled out my treasured felt sleeping bag. I spread it over them, and though Lisa didn't stop sobbing, at least she wasn't trembling any more. Then it occurred to me that kids have to eat. I reached back again and retrieved a tin box of Dutch cookies I had lugged all the way from British Airborne headquarters in Eindhoven in the Netherlands and had been preserving carefully for a special occasion. Lisa ate her cookies ravenously. Freddie wouldn't touch his until he saw me put one into my own mouth.

I went back to studying my maps. The artillery fire, particularly from the east, seemed to be coming closer.

The Battle of the Bulge was under way, but I didn't know it. In retrospect, neither did Eisenhower, Bradley, or Montgomery at that moment; but even if I had been aware of that cosmic fact, it wouldn't have given me much comfort.

I kept staring at the maps and wondering how I—an Army Staff Sergeant who had had the cunning to lick the military system for three years—had got myself into a situation where I was stuck with two kids I didn't understand and in which my cunning was useless.

Until then, with a minimum of hairbreadth escapes, I had

been able to contend with everything the Army had thrown at me. It hadn't taken me more than two days after being drafted to realize that for me, anyway, the enemy was not so much the Nazis as the System. But by now I had learned that no matter how tough and inflexible it seemed, the Army was manipulable. Which is how I managed to get out of the infantry and onto *Yank,* the Army magazine.

Being a combat correspondent wasn't easy, but it beat going to Officer Candidate School and becoming an infantry lieutenant—which is what I had been slated for. As a *Yank* reporter I had managed to survive Omaha Beach, though my photographer, Sgt. Pete Paris, was killed. I'd had some close calls at St.-Lô (where the famous civilian combat artist John Groth did a humiliating nationally circulated sketch of me cowering in a ditch while American bombs fell all around us in the 35th Division area); and at St.-Malo, Nijmegen, and Aachen. Also, because of my fairly fluent French, I had had to put in some time behind the lines with the French and the Belgian resistance forces. But on the whole, even though I still didn't know how to fire a weapon and didn't even carry one, I had learned how to survive—with a lot of help from my friends in various infantry divisions. They got to know my vulnerabilities as well as my by-line and looked after me. I had routinely been promoted to Staff Sergeant by then, and it sometimes embarrassed me when the mortar shells started falling and some division public relations corporal would push me into a slit trench and fall in on top of me to shield me with his own body.

Still, I was alive. I felt guilty when my protectors had to stay there while I, with my own jeep, could flee to the rear as soon as I had my story. The GI's bore me no ill will, however, merely shrugging and saying things like, "Every man for himself." They secretly admired me and the other *Yank* correspondents because we had conned Supreme Headquarters into letting us wear officers' trench coats with civilian correspondent patches on them, which meant that the brass in the field wouldn't withhold information or pull rank on us (not *knowing* our rank). Every time I questioned some Colonel sharply about some boo-boo he might have made, there would be a group of GI's who knew me, smiling appreciatively in the background.

I had now reached December—after having been in the field since D Day in June—and I thought I had it made. The war seemed to be running down. The Army, expecting a complete Nazi collapse, had established a point system based on earned combat stars and medals for the early discharge of line soldiers in the European Theater. Despite my broken-field running across France, Belgium, and Holland, I had accumulated a lot of combat stars and medals. I would be going home soon, I thought.

Until, that is, the night of December 16.

I was in Brussels when it began to happen. Having just undergone the house-to-house fighting in the siege of Aachen, the first city we took in Germany, I had sent my story off via the Press Wireless van in Spa and decided to award myself a vacation. Since I had no immediate officer to whom to report (the closest being at 205 East 42nd Street in New York), I merely got in my jeep and took off.

I went to pass a pleasant three days with Giselle, a girl I had met under a gargoyle in the Grand Place during the liberation of Brussels a few months before by the British—to whom I had attached myself with a set of phony orders. Giselle was a precursor of Women's Lib, a braless beauty who was making her way as a *téléphoniste* for Montgomery's press headquarters and as a student leader for Congolese independence at Louvain University.

Early in the morning after my first night in Giselle's apartment, I was walking around naked while my little Belgian flower was making what passed for coffee and humming snatches of *Oklahoma!,* the score of which she had memorized from a record album I'd brought her from England. Turning

17

on the radio, I came in on the tail end of a BBC agricultural report, followed by the morning news. The more-nasal-than-usual British announcer began with a brief note on the daily communiqué from Supreme Headquarters:

> The American First Army continued its attack into Germany today, in the direction of the Roer Dams. To the South, General Patton's Third Army was poised for an expected new assault into the Saar Region of Germany. On the Ardennes front, there were strong localized enemy attacks, described by the Allied High Command as spoiling operations, but contained by our forces.

What bothered me was not so much the hard facts from the communiqué (the usual mélange of obfuscation) but the more subtle implication that things were heating up; someone might send a Press Wireless query and discover my absence. Also, though I had all my worldly possessions with me in the *Lootwagen,* I had left my typewriter behind in my room at the Hotel du Portugal in Spa, then the 9th Air Force press headquarters. The press camps moved quickly, and if this one pulled out while I was gone, I might lose my typewriter. For a *Yank* correspondent, losing his typewriter was as serious as an infantryman's losing his rifle.

I decided I'd better head back to Spa. Giselle, accustomed to my sudden comings and goings, was unperturbed when I announced my decision. She kissed me, dried a dish, and finished singing "Everything's up-to-date in Kansas City."

It took me eighteen hours to drive the sixty miles from Brussels to Liège, because Route N 3 was clogged with an extraordinary tangle of tanks and trucks, and because of a pleasant side excursion to one of my favorite restaurants near Tirlemont. I turned south on N 15, where the traffic still was bumper to bumper, but after I took the Spa cutoff, the number of military vehicles gradually thinned out to zero. I began to worry about that. I became considerably more worried when I reached Spa. The town was completely deserted. There wasn't a soul, military or civilian, in the usually jammed Place Royale.

I rushed upstairs to my room in the Hôtel du Portugal. It had been completely cleaned out. I looked futilely for my typewriter and then came down again into the empty Place. A woman, about fifty and dressed in peasant black, was standing on the curb alongside my jeep. She had two small children with her. She kept wringing her hands and sending terrified looks over her shoulder.

"Thank God, you've come," she said in French.

"Thank God, *you've* come," I replied. "Where *is* everybody?"

"Gone, all gone. The Boche tanks already are in Francorchamps, taking the American gasoline from the many cans which are stored along the road."

"Then I had better be going too." I climbed into my jeep.

"No, wait," she implored. "You must take these children with you." The children were staring up at me, neither of them saying a word.

"Madame," I said, "I do not understand children. Besides, it is against regulations for civilian personnel to ride in a United States Army vehicle." Knowing the Belgian reverence for regulations, I felt sure that would get the woman off my back.

"No, please, please," she said. "These children are Jews."

2

I had been studying my Michelin Atlas in the courtyard of the church at Theux for about twenty minutes when a young priest with frightened eyes suddenly came out of a side door of the building. Under his black cassock he wore a heavy Norwegian skiing sweater; its gay red reindeer pattern contrasted oddly with the clerical garb. He was carrying two rough mugs of warm milk, steaming in the cold air. He said, "Perhaps the children would like this." Then, with a terrified look in the direction of the distant artillery fire, he put the mugs down on the hood of the jeep and scurried back through the door before I could ask him what was going on.

I gave the milk to Lisa and Freddie, who gulped the creamy liquid down, nestled under my warm felt sleeping bag, and fell asleep. I got out of the jeep and took the two empty mugs over to the little side door through which the priest had materialized. It was locked. I heard the muffled voice of the priest inside. "Just leave the mugs on the door sill, monsieur." Then, pleading, "And please go, monsieur, as quickly as possible. I have fifty old people and children taking refuge in the cellar here, and if the Boches come and see your jeep, they'll think . . ." His voice trailed off.

I went back to the jeep and pulled out a little battery-operated civilian radio. I had liberated it from an apartment

in which I was forced to hole up during the Battle of Aachen.
I set the radio up on the hood and spun the dial to try to pick
up a news broadcast from somewhere. Obviously I was in a
valley; all that came in was Brahms' Third Symphony from
Radio Luxembourg. While I rotated the radio to try for more
volume on another couple of weak signals, I looked through the
windshield: Lisa's head had fallen against Freddie's, and the
two pointy caps were like double inverted exclamation points.
I also noted my own reflection in the windshield: helmeted;
trench-coated; six feet tall; shaken. Well, it was only an hour
since the woman in Spa had begged me to take the children
with me.

I suppose I didn't say anything after she cried out to me
that they were Jews, because she had seized my sleeve and
poured out a torrent of French so fast I could barely follow it.
"But you don't understand, monsieur, these children are Jews
from Germany. Their father and mother were gassed in a con-
centration camp, but some Christian neighbors hid the children from the Gestapo. For two years, monsieur, these children
were passed from family to family all across Germany until
they reached Aachen. There my sister cared for them. When
your American Army captured Aachen, my sister brought them
across the border to me, here in Belgium, thinking they at last
would be safe. But now, monsieur," she was crying, "now, if
the SS come and then the Gestapo . . ."

"O.K.," I said, "put them in the jeep. I'll take them as far
as the nearest Red Cross girl." The woman lifted the kids into
the front seat and then embarrassed me by dropping to her
knees and kissing my paratrooper boots.

"Please contain yourself, madame," I said. And, to get things
back on an even keel, "What are the names of these children?"

She had already begun to run across the square in the
direction of the Imperial Bath House, where Kaiser Wilhelm
once took the cure, but she stopped to call over her shoulder:
"The children have had many names, but when they came to

my sister they were known as Lisa and Friedrich Westermann. God bless you, monsieur." Whereupon she disappeared into one of the many ground-floor entrances of the Bath House.

"Sure, God bless me," I grumbled as I kept rotating the radio atop the hood of the jeep. Finally I removed it from the hood and took it a few steps away from the metal of the vehicle. Almost immediately I heard the strains of "Lili Marlene," a song played almost incessantly on the German State Radio. Then came the unmistakable voice of Axis Sally:

> The Fuehrer today personally announced a grand offensive designed to divide the enemy forces and to drive to the sea at Antwerp. The operation, code-name "Westwind," began yesterday, designated as "Null-Day" by the Fuehrer, and already has achieved notable success. The enemy lines have been seriously breached by our Panzer divisions in the area of Losheim and the Schnee Eifel on the border between the Reich and the Grand Duchy of Luxembourg.

I didn't believe the Kraut communiqué any more than I had the Allied one I heard in Giselle's apartment, but now at least I knew the general area where the action was going on. Both Losheim and the Schnee Eifel were to the south and east. Therefore, I reasoned, I could head northeast to Eupen. The First Division was in a rest area there, and attached to the division was a lovely Red Cross girl with whom I knew I could dump the kids and then look out for myself.

I got back to the jeep and started the engine. The children stirred sleepily but didn't wake up. I drove to the outskirts of Verviers, where Route N 31 would take me directly to Eupen. But at the crossroads of N 31 and N 27, someone had taken down the road signs. Before I knew it, I was on N 27—heading toward Malmédy.

It was the first of several serious mistakes I was to make in the next few days.

3

After seven months of darting in and out of combat, I had developed a pretty good knowledge of the symptoms of inadvertent straying from friendly into unfriendly territory.

First, there were the cows.

When people fight a modern war in civilized agricultural countries, a lot of innocent cows get killed—usually by the concussion of exploding artillery shells. This bothered me because I've always liked cows.

Dead cows bloat up, even in winter, and they lie on their backs, all four feet extended stiffly in the air. Also, dead cows smell—fearsomely. The smell is not unlike that of dead people. Thus, when our GI's dug in to occupy a field or a patch of woods in Europe, the first thing they'd do after the Graves Registration troops removed the dead *people* was remove the neighboring dead *cows*. They cut the fresh ones into steaks and ate them. To get rid of the dreadful stench of the riper cows, they would call in a bulldozer from a supporting tank unit. The bulldozer, sometimes just a blade attached to the front of a tank, would dig a deep trench, push the cows in, and then bury them. The Germans did the same thing on their side. Therefore, if you passed through an area of no dead cows and suddenly found yourself in an area where they were all over the place, you worried.

You also looked for telephone lines. Since, even with radio, every unit was connected by telephone line to its fellow units and higher headquarters, the European roadsides proliferated with a multi-hued tangle of telephone lines—usually strung out on the ground like never-ending elongated flower patches, but occasionally hanging garland-fashion from fences. Horrifyingly, upright frozen corpses were known to be used by the Signal Corps as temporary posts to support their precious wires. When you saw no telephone wires along a road, that meant there were no more front-line units and you were in trouble. When you saw no more telephone lines and a lot of dead cows, that meant *real* trouble.

It had happened to me near St.-Lô in Normandy—before I had learned the significance of cows and lines. Turning a sharp corner in the jeep, I had suddenly found myself looking into the eyes of a Kraut manning an 88 on a half-track before I realized where I was and skidded into a U-turn and back down the road. The Kraut didn't fire at me; either he was too amused, or his side's ammunition was so short at the time that a single jeep didn't seem to be a worth-while target.

Now, I felt reassured. As I blundered down the road to Malmédy with Lisa and Freddie, there were plenty of telephone wires and no dead cows. Eventually I found myself in Malmédy, a pretty country town set on rolling hills, where I was further reassured by the presence of the vehicles of the 291st Combat Engineer Battalion, a seasoned outfit I knew well. There even was an MP directing traffic.

Though I now realized my mistake, I decided to continue on through the narrow clogged streets of Malmédy and double back to Eupen via a crossroads at Baugnez, a couple of miles further on. Five roads converged at Baugnez, where there was a pleasant little café called the Bodarwé at which I had drunk a lot of good Belgian beer. I also remembered the Baugnez crossroads from a previous occasion when I had passed there with a blond lady photographer named Lee Miller, who was a war correspondent for, of all publications, *Vogue*. A perspiring MP had been busy disentangling five streams of military vehicles at the junction when Miss Miller asked him how to get to Bastogne. Continuing to wave his arms at the onrushing trucks and tanks, he'd said, "It beats the shit out of me, Mac." Then, looking down and seeing Lee's officer's uniform, he said, "Excuse me. It beats the shit out of me, *ma'am*."

Now, just before I reached Baugnez, I recognized the telltale signs. The telephone lines were ripped up. There was the smell of dead cows—or dead people, I couldn't tell which. In the rapidly falling dusk, I could see a smoldering ruin where the Café Bodarwé had been.

I stopped the jeep to try to turn around. The sudden braking awakened Lisa and Freddie, who looked up at me, startled. I found that I couldn't turn around; both sides of the road were jammed with wrecked, burned-out U.S. Army trucks.

At that moment I peered ahead through the growing darkness and the mist and saw a military convoy approaching from the east and turning south at the crossroads. "Thank God," I said to myself and took the jeep forward again. I eased myself into the convoy behind another jeep. As we shot past the still-glowing remains of the Café Bodarwé, I caught a glimpse of what seemed to be a lot of bundles of clothes lying in the snow-covered field beyond it.

I traveled with the convoy for a mile or two, inching along, like the others, with my headlights out. It was getting so dark that I had to strain to follow the white U.S. Army star on the jeep ahead of me. Everything seemed to be fine until the children began to cry softly. I thought Lisa had to go to the bathroom again, but she just pointed to the truck behind us. The soldiers in the back of the truck were singing. I didn't see anything unusual about that until I concentrated on the sound.

The singing was in German.

I switched on my blue black-out lights for an instant and stared at the white-starred jeep in front of me. The four soldiers

27

in it were wearing Kraut helmets. It must be a *captured* American jeep.

And I must be wandering along in the middle of a German Army convoy.

By now the sweat was turning to hoarfrost on my face. I pushed the kids to the floor so their silhouettes wouldn't show and kept looking to the side of the road, searching for a gap in the forest where I might swerve off. Finally I decided to swerve off anyway—as if I had to stop to take a leak. It meant running the risk of being crashed into by the three-ton truck behind me, but I swerved.

I bumped along the shoulder of the road for a few feet and then, miraculously, made out a less dark opening in the forest. It was a firebreak road between the carefully planted rows of firs whose faggots had heated Belgian houses for generations. I pulled into the firebreak as slowly and as nonchalantly as I could. I winced, waiting for the reaction of gunfire.

The convoy just kept rolling on—toward Ligneuville.

Moving in the darkness at about two miles an hour and using my four-wheel drive in the two-inch-deep snow, I gradually pushed a half mile or so into the forest. Then I literally collapsed, not really collecting myself until I felt a warm mitten pressed anxiously against my cheek. It was Lisa's.

I don't know how long I sat there. All I remember is that after a while I became conscious of an inordinate amount of squirming and giggling going on under the sleeping bag beside me. The kids were wide awake now, babbling away in German and poking and jostling each other like a couple of kittens. I couldn't understand how people—even children—could react so lightheartedly after what we had just been through. Which only seemed to remind me of how little I knew about kids.

"Shhh!" I said. The squirming and giggling stopped abruptly, and I felt guilty about shutting them up so sharply.

I lit my Zippo lighter, carefully shielding the flame with my gloved hand as I foraged in the back of the jeep for some food. The first thing that came within range was a case of K-rations, and I pulled out two of the dreadful little cardboard packages. The kids ate the chocolate. I contented myself with the small cans of meat that always, somehow, reminded me of dog food.

When we had finished eating, I flicked the Zippo to light one of the off-brand cigarettes (I think these were Wings) that were provided in the U.S. Army K-ration package by our free-enterprise system. It was then that I saw something in the flicker of light cast by the Zippo—and the sweat poured out again, just as it had back on the road.

There was a man standing in the woods, maybe ten feet from the jeep. He had his hands raised above his head and he was saying something: "*Uebergabe.*"

I doused the light, as if hoping he was an apparition that would go away. Another "*Uebergabe*" came weakly out of the darkness.

After a reasonable interval for panic-suppression, I lit the Zippo once more and held it up to take a better look at the man. He had moved a few feet closer. I now could see clearly that he was wearing a U.S. Army uniform. The overcoat, a long jagged tear showing from the hem to the waist, bore the shoulder patch of the First Army.

"Why the hell are you surrendering to *me,* you silly son-of-a-bitch? I'm an American, just like you."

The man seemed almost disappointed. He sank to his haunches in the snow and said, "Mother-fuck this fuckin' war." Then he looked up brightly at me and asked, "You got any cognac in that mother-fuckin' heap of yours?"

I reached back and recognized, by touch, a bottle of Remy Martin. I grabbed it, along with my flashlight, and squatted down in the snow alongside the GI, partly covering the light with my helmet. We each took a long pull at the Remy Martin bottle. In the glow I could see that my companion was tall, scrawny, and red-faced. A lock of sand-colored hair hung over his forehead. The children had fallen silent when they heard that first word in German, but now they resumed talking to each other. "Christ," the GI said, "you got kids in that jeep?" The accent was Tennessee or North Georgia, tempered with a little Midwest Big City, possibly Detroit.

I mumbled my implausible explanation of the children's presence. The GI just shrugged and, taking another swig, said, "Well, whaddaya expect? In a Tarfu like this, nothin' surprises me."

(Tarfu, a word coined around the time of the Battle of the Bulge, was a superlative developed from the GI expression Snafu—Situation Normal, All Fucked Up. Tarfu was the acronym for Things Are *Really* Fucked Up. An even stronger superlative was Fubar—Fucked Up Beyond All Recognition.)

"Speaking of Tarfu," I said, "what are you doing out here alone in the woods trying to surrender?"

"Christ, man, I nearly got my ass shot off yesterday like them other poor bastards back at the crossroads." I remembered those "bundles of clothes" spilled in the field alongside the burned café at Baugnez.

"What happened?"

"It was a fuckin' massacre, that's what happened," he said, and proceeded to give me a first-hand account of what later did come to be called the Malmédy Massacre.

He told me he had been sent back in a jeep by his company commander in the 106th Division at the front to pick up some mail and maps at a depot in Ligneuville. On the way, he decided to tarry at the Café Bodarwé (which he referred to as the Bide-a-wee) for the purpose of obtaining "a piece" from a barmaid he knew at the tavern.

"I sat there with her in the back room the whole fuckin' mornin'," he said. "She was as useless to me as a one-legged man at an ass-kickin'. She spent all our time watchin' the

30

Seventh Fuckin' Armored Division go through, on the north-to-south road. Then there was a gap in the traffic and the MP who was directin' traffic took off in his jeep. Right after that, another outfit come down the road. From what I could see on their trucks, they were Battery B of the 285th Fuckin' Field Artillery Observation Battalion. I looked up then and I nearly shit when I seen a Kraut armored column comin' down to the crossroads from the east. The biggest fuckin' tanks I ever seen in my life. They opened up on the artillery guys and it was no contest. They hit most of the artillery guys' trucks, and the whole fuckin' outfit surrendered. They had their hands over their heads, and the Krauts took their pieces away and moved them into the field behind the café."

While the GI (by now I knew his name was Chick) refreshed himself with another swig from the bottle, I tried to remember what I knew of the 285th Field Artillery Observation Battalion. A week or two earlier, I had taken a meal with them near Spa. They were a freshly arrived unit, lightly armed, and trained to do forward spotting for the big guns. They had seen no combat up to that point. I recalled joking with a kid named Phil Davidson about whether or not we were related.

Chick swallowed more brandy, asked me for a cigarette, and continued: "Anyway, these artillery ass-holes was millin' around the field, and they was laughin' and kiddin' like it's a big fuckin' joke. The next thing I know, a Kraut half-track comes along in the column and the Krauts in the half-track open up on the guys in the field with a .50 calibre machine gun. Then the other Krauts start firin' their fuckin' grease guns. Then a couple of Kraut officers go in the field with the Lugers and shoot all the artillery guys who are still movin'. It was a fuckin' mess. I threw up all over the back room of the café and then I hauled my ass outta there. I crawled to the woods and when I looked back, they had set the fuckin' café on fire too."

I whistled. "Do you know what Kraut outfit it was?"

"SS," Chick said. "While I was crawlin' down the ditch to

the woods, I seen the tanks had the two lightnin' flashes on them and the word 'Peiper.' What the fuck does *that* mean?"

I whistled again. From my research for a story on the Red Army, I knew that Obersturmbannfuehrer (Lieutenant Colonel) Jochen Peiper had led SS tank task forces which had committed some of the worst atrocities of the war on the Russian Front. He was of such ill repute in the East that the Russians had offered the Order of Lenin or such to anyone who took him alive. If the Krauts had moved Peiper to the Western Front, something big *must* be going on.

I told Chick, who said, predictably, "Let's get the fuck outta here."

4

We moved tne jeep further down the firebreak to a nice, comfortable, branch-camouflaged hole Chick had dug for himself. It was well stocked with canned goodies he had managed to carry away with him from the café's back room—even in his precipitous flight.

I was beginning to like Chick. He was surprisingly gentle with the children, feeding them some smoked trout from his private stock, helping them to wash with snow melted in his helmet, tucking them in warmly again in the jeep. Also, in his own fashion, he was as cynical about the Army as I was.

He had landed in Normandy with the 29th Division but soon conned himself into a job driving for a Lieutenant Colonel at Corps Headquarters and then at Supreme Headquarters in Versailles. He was shipped out to the newly formed 106th Division only because, as he put it, "I got caught playing around with the Colonel's personal nookie." He already was working himself back into a driving job at Corps when he found himself in the contretemps at Baugnez.

In a strange way, he reminded me of *me*—and, as we drank, I found myself telling him about my *own* military career.

I had been drafted not long after graduating from New York University. In college I had earned a Bachelor's degree with a major in English, and a boxful of medals for running the high and low hurdles better than a lot of other people in intercollegiate track competition.

The medals turned out to be more valuable than the English major. In a depressed market, they helped get me writing assignments from magazine editors who formerly had admired my atrocious but winning form over the hurdles and somehow thought that heightened my expertise as a sports writer. Along with articles for the magazines, I also ended up writing lies, in the guise of "sports legends," for Bill Stern of NBC, a noted sportscaster of that day. One of my most famous lies, disseminated by Stern over 300-odd radio stations, was Abraham Lincoln's deathbed scene, in which I had the assassinated President regain consciousness for a moment and say to Secretary of War Stanton, "Tell Abner Doubleday, don't let baseball die."

I had just finished making up a whopper about a Finnish javelin thrower hurling a sapling loaded with grenades into an enemy headquarters during the Russo-Finnish War when my induction notice arrived from the draft board. As anti-Nazi as anybody, I went off to Fort Dix without too much protest. I wasn't at Fort Dix more than two days before I set about devising ways of beating the military system.

As a former sports writer (dispatched by my press colleagues with a memorable carouse before I departed to participate in the glorious defense of the homeland), I was sentimentally added to a permanent list for receiving complimentary tickets to the Friday night Madison Square Garden fights and to all games of the New York Yankees and Giants and the Brooklyn Dodgers. After my first day of latrine duty in the Army, I looked around to see where my freebees would do me the most good. I discovered that the First Sergeant of my Reception Company was a rabid boxing fan. One freebee a week to Madison Square Garden miraculously kept me out of the latrine— as well as off all KP and guard duty.

Next I located a Captain in G-1 (Personnel) who was wild

34

for the Giants. A freebee a week to him not only got me off shipping lists to Fort Benning and and other infantry training centers, but when the Captain was assigned to First Army Headquarters on Governors Island in New York Harbor he had me sent there, too, in order to insure his uninterrupted flow of box seats at the Polo Grounds and, when the Giants were playing, at Ebbetts Field.

At Governors Island I found there was no post newspaper, so I immediately volunteered to write, edit, and publish one. My grateful Colonel (a Yankee fan) immediately provided me with a room, a typewriter, and a duplicating machine—and saw to it that I was not bothered with such formalities as basic training. I made up most of the stories in my newspaper, quaintly named *The Reveille Gun,* adding just enough truth to flatter the brass. My talent for fabrication apparently caught the eye of the Colonel, name of Ed Glavin, who was in charge of public relations for the First Army, and I was transferred to an office in Lower Manhattan.

At 90 Church Street I did such things as ghost a history of World War II to that date, for the Encyclopedia Britannica. The signature that appeared on the history was that of Lieutenant General Hugh Drum, Commander of the First Army. I was able to convince my immediate superior, Major Bates Raney (a Dodger fan) that such scholarly research required much work at night in the public library, and he gave me permission to live in my own Manhattan apartment instead of in the Governors Island barracks. I still hadn't been taught how to fire a weapon but I was promoted to Corporal.

I suffered a temporary setback to my comfort when I was forced to go on maneuvers in North and South Carolina, but it was World Series time and a block of Yankee Stadium tickets distributed to a certain Lieutenant Colonel at least got me out of a tent and into a room (albeit in the servants' quarters) of a Camden, South Carolina, hotel. My job was to wander around the mock battlefield and to assist the civilian radio correspondents in gathering news of the "war" between the First Army and the Third Army.

One day I witnessed the ignominious capture of our First Army Commander, General Drum, by some Third Army MP's, on whom the General attempted to pull rank to induce them to forget the shameful incident. The incident amused me and I reported it to a friend of mine, Bill Slocum of CBS, who in turn reported it—with colorful detail—over his entire radio network. The merriment caused by this national disclosure may have been one reason why Drum *didn't* get the job as Supreme Commander, for which he had been slated rather than Dwight D. Eisenhower. I felt sorry for Drum, but not for long. He came out of the National Guard with all its politics. Besides, he never even hinted that maybe I should have an acknowledgment on the Encyclopedia Britannica history I had written for him.

Soon thereafter (possibly because someone in Washington appreciated this course of events), I received a mysterious set of orders directing me to report to a military base I never had heard of—205 East 42nd Street, New York, N.Y. I arrived at the skyscraper address, barracks bag on my shoulder, to find a huge office furnished with about a hundred desks and typewriters, and populated with just two disreputable-looking GI's sitting around playing draw poker. They were Marion Hargrove and a former Yale poet named Harry Brown.

Both were as mystified as I was about why we were there. So I joined the card game and in about three days, a jaunty-looking Captain bounced in and introduced himself as Hartzell Spence, the novelist. He regarded us with some distaste and then informed us that we were the vanguard of a new Army magazine to be known as *Yank*.

On *Yank*, after the rest of the 100-odd man staff drifted in, I found a lot of kindred spirits. We did have a few gung-ho soldiers, but most of us were displaced civilian-journalist misfits on whom the Army had not quite succeeded in rubbing off. We all were enlisted men (so the GI's would believe what we wrote), and the few officers who were sent in to administer

36

us—but not to tell us what to do editorially—were as desultory as we were about military procedure.

We wrote and edited our magazine, and generally we were left alone. From time to time, however, our free-spirit manner perturbed the outside brass, and tough Regular Army First Sergeants were sent in to instill some measure of military discipline in us. It usually turned out that the topkicks fell into our libertarian ways, instead of vice versa, and found themselves transferred elsewhere.

For a while I traveled around the United States reporting on our men in training for the upcoming assaults on Africa, Europe, and the South Pacific. I also dreamed up a series that I thought would keep me out of the storm's eye for an indefinite period: "Home Towns in Wartime." It worked, but only for a few months. *Someone* had to go to England to beef up our pre-D Day staff there, and I was the one.

In England, I flew combat missions over Occupied Europe with the Eighth Air Force—but as infrequently as possible. I became expert at concocting exotic assignments which took me elsewhere, such as "The Red Army Man," "The Secret War in the Congo," and "On Anti E-Boat Patrol With the British Navy in the North Sea."

With D Day, such escape routes were cut off for me. But I still managed to get by with a minimum of exposure to danger—as had my new-found friend, Chick, until happenstance brought us together near the scene of the Malmédy Massacre.

I looked over at Chick, who had fallen asleep from the effects of the cognac and was snoring loudly by the time I had come to the end of my story. I shook him awake. "Let's go," I said.

"Go *where?*"

"It's only seven o'clock and plenty dark. I think we can drive the jeep down the firebreak until we come to another road and get around the Krauts."

"Fuck you," he said. "I'm staying here."

"What are you going to do?"

A sly smile came over his face. "I'll tell ya what I'm gonna do. I'm gonna stay here in my little ole hole and I'm gonna wait till I hear sputterin' and moanin' from the Kraut column back there on the road. That'll mean the SS has gone on and the Volksgrenadier trucks is follerin' them up. The Volksgrenadiers allus follers the SS. Them Volksgrenadiers is nice old men from the Home Guard who don't like fightin' any more'n I do. So I'm gonna find myself a gentle old Volksgrenadier and then I'm gonna surrender to him. That's what I thought *you* was when you come down the firebreak."

I couldn't help smiling at his pragmatism. "Well," I said, "*I've* got to get going with these kids, so at least tell me what you know about the military situation."

He bent down to draw a crude map on the snow. "Wal," he said, "from what I picked up when I drove back here yesterday, the Krauts broke through them two new ass-hole divisions, the 106th and the 99th. It looks to me like we got two good divisions they'll have a peck of trouble bustin' into. That's the First, up here in the north, and the Fourth, down around Echternach in Luxembourg.

"So if I was you, I'd foller the firebreaks and take the back roads headin' south, till you figger you're behind the Fourth Division." He grinned and pointed toward the sound of Panzers, still, apparently, approaching the Baugnez crossroads from the direction of Germany. "Seems like ya got no choice," he said, "seein' as them double-lightnin's got you blocked off to the north."

I got into the jeep without waking the children and turned on the motor. "How soon do you think the Volksgrenadiers will come for you?" I asked.

"Beats the shit outta me, Mac," he said and lowered himself into his well-camouflaged hole.

5

It took me nearly an hour just to get out of Chick's woods. The firebreak ended less than a half mile from his hole. I had to pick my way along the rows of carefully spaced firs, using my blue black-out lights on the jeep. Thank God for the well-ordered minds of the Belgians. There was just enough room between the rows of trees to allow a wagon—or a small vehicle —through. If they had been planted helter-skelter, like the French trees, I never would have gotten out of the woods. Also, as early practitioners of ecology, the Belgians had planted new young trees every few hundred yards or so, where a section of the old ones had been cut and their stumps removed. I regretted damaging the seedlings as I rode over them, but these sections of the forest were easy to traverse.

The children were chattering and wriggling as I navigated. They had slept most of the time since I had inherited them early that afternoon, and now they were as active as nocturnal hamsters who wake in their cages every evening and then spend the night running in their exercise wheels. Maybe these kids are nocturnal creatures, I thought, considering the amount of night-time traveling they must have done while they were being smuggled out of Germany.

As I strained to peer ahead into the darkness, I was only half listening to their Kraut talk, but then I heard something that made me pay closer attention—both Lisa and Freddie were attempting to repeat some of the saltier expressions in Chick's dialogue. "Fuckintank," said Lisa, giggling. "Muzzerfuckin," said Freddie, giggling back.

I was appalled. I don't know why. Perhaps it was some still unborn paternalism within me, but I didn't like the idea of *my* kids—however temporary—saying things like that, even though they didn't understand the words. I tried to think back to advice-to-parents columns I'd come across in my newspaper reading. I seemed to recall that it was best to ignore the dirty-word syndrome rather than to encourage or inhibit a child by making too much of it.

So I ignored it for a while, but when delicate little Lisa said "muzzerfuckin," I couldn't stand it any longer. I stopped the jeep and roared at them: *"Nicht sagen das* 'mother-fuckin.' *Is* naughty, bad, *schlecht."* The children lapsed into silence the moment I raised my voice. Then Freddie asked, *"Schlecht?"* *"Ya,"* I said, *"schlecht, schlecht,* you little sons-of-bitches." There was another moment of silence while they obviously pondered the reasons for my wrath. I started the jeep again. "Sombishes," Freddie piped up. "Sombishes," echoed Lisa. *"Nein, nein, nein,"* I said, *"das* also *is schlecht."*

It went on like that for quite some time, but I was heartened by the fact that we were beginning to communicate.

I decided I'd better watch my *own* language—what with two eager young parrots being around—but it wasn't long before I slipped again.

It happened just after we left Chick's woods, crossed a deserted country road, and entered another fir forest via a firebreak. I stopped the jeep to try to check my bearings with a small compass I had found in one of the compartments of the vehicle. The halt, apparently, was what Freddie had been waiting for.

I had noticed him casting curious glances into the back of the jeep from which, he had learned, all blessings flowed. While

I was out of the jeep studying the compass with my shielded flashlight, he crawled into the *Lootwagen* to explore By the time I turned the light on the *Lootwagen* to see what was going on, he had done some pretty good rooting around. In fact, he came up with his head stuck through the middle of one of my prized possessions: the Throne.

The Throne was a cane-seated chair I had found in a farmhouse at St. Sauveur Lendelin, just beyond the Omaha Beach unpleasantness. After three days of squatting down in an open field I had decided there was a better way to move one's bowels in wartime. The answer was the Throne. I took the chair, cut away the cane seat, and shortened the legs five inches or so. I then could dig a small hole, sit comfortably on the Throne after positioning it over the hole, and even preserve daintiness by kicking dirt in the hole upon completion. No one touched the Throne, except for front-line GI's to whom I occasionally lent it in the field.

And here was Freddie, pealing with laughter, his head protruding through what had been the cane bottom of the sacred object. Lisa was laughing too. I extricated Freddie from the Throne and snarled, "Kid, you're a pain in the ass." That was a mistake. Lisa took up my words and began singing them like a jump-rope chant: "Friedrich *bist ein* pain in der ass, Friedrich *bist ein* pain in der ass."

At that point, I realized it was going to be impossible to keep their newly acquired vocabulary clean. So I gave up.

Fearing that the children's noise might attract any Krauts who might be in the neighborhood, I quieted them with another ferocious-sounding "Sh!" and resumed our odyssey.

I began to make better time. After crossing several roads and finding them devoid of people—even Belgians—I realized that I could use the back-country lanes and not be bound to the woods. I kept heading in a generally southeasterly direction. We passed farmhouses and even little hamlets that looked so normal—lamplight even showed through the shutters—that the war could have been a thousand miles away. I *did* take to the woods again, but only to bypass the more sizable towns (German-sounding ones with names like Buchholz and Honsfeld) where I figured the onrushing Krauts might have left garrisons behind them.

Actually, for four hours, we didn't see a living human being.

How could this happen, with nearly a million men involved in a major military offensive?

This war, I had learned, was nothing like what we read in print or saw on film. We had been conditioned, I suppose, by the literature and movies about World War I, which *was* a static conflict—with enormous masses of men and equipment lined up against each other across hundreds of miles of front. Except for a few instances, such as the Nazis' attempts to contain us in the Normandy beachhead and our own assaults on Germany's Westwall, World War II was nothing like that.

It was mainly a war of movement. Comparatively small units would blunder and probe in various directions; occasionally they would make contact, and there would be a battle. When the battle was equally fought, both sides would bring up reinforcements and there would be a major battle, temporarily, from fixed positions. The rest of the time, the countryside was a hodgepodge of pockets of war and peace. On the Normandy beachhead, for example, Caen was devastated; neighboring Bayeux was untouched. In the Battle of the Bulge, as I learned later, the war swirled all around Malmédy—coming within two miles of it at the Baugnez crossroads—but the town was as unaffected as it had been in the days of Louis IV. Until, that is, it was flattened by our 9th Air Force, which mistook it for a town in Germany.

Obersturmbannfuehrer Peiper, the spearhead of the entire German Sixth Panzer Army, came within a hundred yards of the town of Trois Ponts. But when he couldn't get his 60-ton Royal Tiger tanks across a bridge over the Salm River, he veered north to La Gleize. La Gleize eventually looked as if an earthquake had leveled it. In Trois Ponts, less than five miles away, the people ate normally, played, worked, looked after their cattle and tended the seventh-century abbey which is the town's principal tourist attraction.

So there were great gaps—especially out in the fields and woods—where absolutely nothing was happening, and the war could have been as far away as Stalingrad. It was not too different from the Battle of Hastings in 1066, during which the entire fate of England was settled, while just over the hill shepherds tended their flocks as if nothing at all were going on.

There were two factors that contributed to this peculiar situation in the Battle of the Bulge. For one thing, so-called Intelligence on both sides was deplorable. With our Air Forces and the Luftwaffe hampered by the weather, often nobody knew where the other side was. Deadly armored columns kept moving around without making contact with each other— until specific fronts finally became defined at such places as Bastogne and St. Vith. A perfect example of the great empty spaces that existed between the contending forces was what the newspapers described as "the historic link-up between the Third and the First Armies." The historic link-up consisted of two men, Major Michael Greene and Lieutenant Eugene Ellison, walking into the Belgian town of Houffalize. They had led a lone, lightly armored company on a ten-mile all-night march up a back road, without encountering a single German soldier in the gap between the two American armies.

Another thing that limited the active battle area was the fact that both sides were road-bound. The Germans' main objective was to break through to the comparatively flat country beyond La Roche, where they could roll across the open fields in their tanks. Most of them never got that far. They were confined to the hilly, forested Ardennes with its few good highways, which sometimes twisted around hairpin turns the Tigers could not negotiate. Neither could our Sherman tanks, which similarly held to the paved roads to avoid getting bogged down in the dense woods, precipitous canyons, and churned-up fields.

One of the few times the Krauts tried to get through the firebreaks and the country lanes, as I did, they moved only half a mile and then had to turn back, losing precious time. It happened on the second day of the battle, in the Germans' fruitless dash to try to capture the vital bridges over the Salm River in Trois Ponts. If they had pushed on through the woods just another mile or so they would have burst into the open before Trois Ponts could be defended, with a clear path to the Meuse River and Antwerp, beyond. If Peiper had realized this, the war would have gone on for months longer and our side might even have lost it.

So the armored columns of both sides clanked up and down the roads; and at night, especially, you could hear them from two miles away. That's why there wasn't much element of surprise after the shock of the Germans' initial unexpected attack. That's why, too, it wasn't so difficult to find those inactive empty spaces between the contending forces.

Which is what I tried to do most of that night of December 18.

Twice, I nearly found myself in the military traffic again. The first time I had been twisting around on one of the back roads, maneuvering through stone-house hamlets only a mile or two apart. I had just come through what seemed to be a deserted town when I heard the clanking.

I braked to a stop behind an ancient barn and peeked around the corner. Just ahead, about half a mile away, was one of the main east-west roads. On it I could see a steady procession of dim blue black-out headlights. The convoy was moving from east to west, so I figured it had to be the Krauts pushing from behind the Westwall in Germany and into Belgium.

I slammed the jeep in reverse and followed the lane back

44

to a fork I remembered. I took the left fork instead of the right one, as I had done the first time. The lane meandered around for another mile or so. Then, the clanking again. I realized at that point that *all* the back roads must empty into the main one—and that I was trapped.

I sat for a while, considering Chick's theory of surrender. The sound of the convoy had made the children quiet and apprehensive again, but I was more aware of them than when they had been making noise. I could put up with spending the rest of the war in a nice quiet Stalag, but how about them? I was still thinking about those gentle old Volksgrenadiers and the possibility that maybe they wouldn't turn the kids over to the SS or the Gestapo, when something totally unexpected happened.

From where I was watching in the woods near the highway, I heard the rumble and grinding of a tank unit going past. Then the roar of maybe a half-dozen motorcycles (probably Kraut MP's). Then silence.

Not complete silence, because there was another clanking in the east—but it was perhaps half a mile away. I suddenly remembered that in our military convoys, too, there were occasional intervals. The motorcycles could have been the rear escort of one battalion. The following battalion, with its advance escort of MP's on motorcycles, could have been delayed slightly by a broken-down vehicle that had to be pushed off to the side of the road.

I didn't wait to theorize about it any longer. I gunned the jeep down the lane and zoomed across the highway, just as another cluster of blue headlights came around a bend in the road to the east.

The second time I reached a main east-west road, I knew better what to do. I hung back in a firebreak in the woods, waiting for the same inevitable break in the traffic. This time, however, I waited—and sweated—for more than an hour. But finally it came, and I had made it again.

What I didn't know until much later was that the first convoy I traversed was American—the remains of the shattered 106th Division, pulling back to St. Vith from its breached positions in the Schnee Eifel. Had I simply joined in with them, I would have been safely behind U.S. lines by morning. But I didn't know that at the time. I also didn't know that the second armored column I crossed was the dreaded Nazi Panzer Lehr Division.

There were no more big east-west roads and finally, at about 4 A.M., I figured I was far enough south to be behind our Fourth Division. I began to use my flashlight for quick glimpses at the side of the road, searching for the tell-tale telephone lines. I didn't see any.

But suddenly there was a farmhouse, its lighted windows unshuttered. Only Americans would do that, I thought. I pulled into the hay-strewn farmyard and, sure enough, there was an enormous-looking GI with a rifle, ordering me to halt. I nearly cried with relief. In the reflection of the beam cast by his flashlight, I could see the four-leaf-clover Fourth Division patch on his shoulder.

He asked me the password, but I never bothered with such nonsense. "What outfit of the Fourth is this?" I asked.

He grinned foolishly, and I got the distinct impression that he was drunk.

"Welcome to Schloss Hemingstein," he said.

6

I sagged emotionally. I knew all about Schloss Hemingstein. *Schloss* means "castle" in German, and "Hemingstein" is what Ernest Hemingway called himself derogatorily, as when he signed himself "E. Cantwrite Hemingstein." A couple of months earlier, there had been a lot of snickering in the press camps about the fact that the great writer—apparently still trying to re-live his combat days in the Spanish Civil War—had established himself in a farmhouse in the then quiet Ardennes sector. The stories had it that a lot of literature-minded GI's had gone AWOL from their outfits to sit at the feet of the master in the farmhouse; and that Hemingway had organized them into what he called "Hemingway's Irregulars," posting them into squads and sending them out on patrols as if he were their guerrilla leader.

Before that, after the Allied breakthrough at St.-Lô, Hemingway had gotten into trouble by calling himself a Colonel in the FFI (French Forces of the Interior—the Underground) and leading a group of Resistance fighters in actual combat with the fleeing Germans at Rambouillet. Under the terms of the Geneva Convention, war correspondents—and Hemingway was accredited to *Collier's* Magazine—are not supposed to bear arms or participate physically in military actions. It was well known that early in October Hemingway had had to leave

Schloss Hemingstein because of a set of orders he had received directing him to stand trial, in effect, before the Inspector General of Patton's Third Army. He was charged with removing his correspondent's patch, acting as a Colonel in the FFI, commanding troops in combat operations, and owning a personal supply of "grenades, mines, bazookas, and sundry small arms." Somehow, he beat the rap, and the last I'd heard, he had gone back to his favorite sulking place, the Ritz Bar in Paris.

"Is Mr. Hemingway in there?" I asked the stoned guard in the farmyard.

The GI was offended. "You mean *Colonel* Hemingway? Yes, sir. He's in there."

I got the children out of the jeep—the guard was so out-of-it he didn't even notice them—and walked over to the farmhouse door. On the way, I weighed my mixed feelings about being there. On the one hand, I was comforted by the knowledge that at last I was with some people who were on our side. On the other, I doubted if Hemingway knew what the fuck he was doing out there in the middle of nowhere. Nor did I know how he would react to my children. I had previously heard him refer to some of the Jewish war correspondents as "kikes," and I was in no mood to tolerate his anti-Semitism, real or feigned, now.

Like all young writers of my generation, I had grown up idolizing the man. These feelings held up when I first met him during the days of the wild dash from Avranches to Paris after the breakthrough at St.-Lô. He seemed to be the embodiment of the heroic Robert Jordan in *For Whom the Bell Tolls*, his most recent book and one which I had practically memorized.

But then came a nasty incident at Mont-St.-Michel where he used the word "kike" too freely and one of them knocked him on his ass down a flight of ancient stone steps. After that, when I met him at the various press camps, I noticed that he used the word a lot and also referred to even the most heroic black soldiers as "shines." He was drunk practically every time I saw him and frequently complained of being sick with a cold or some such. Although I never was with him in the field, I have no doubt that he exhibited commendable bravery under fire—as he claimed, and as other observers since have corroborated—but his Boy Scout bravado got to me after a while. The war, with all its horror, seemed to be a game to him, and it turned me off when he swaggered around with a Thompson submachine gun and handgrenades hanging from him like Christmas tree ornaments.

By the same token, I felt great sadness about what was happening to him. Once, at the Hotel Brasseur in Luxembourg, he said to me, "Kid, when you're a writer and you can't write, you're like a stud horse without balls." The writing seemed to be coming more and more painfully for him. I occasionally saw some of the stuff he was filing for *Collier's*, and most of it was juvenile crap. Having latched on to the 22nd Regiment of the Fourth Division, he was writing about them as if they were eighteenth-century Three-Musketeers-type cardboard cutouts, instead of the competent professionals in killing they actually were. It devastated him that his estranged wife Martha Gellhorn actually was doing a better job for the same magazine, and that he had so been informed by Charles Colbaugh, an exasperated *Collier's* editor.

His personal life, too, was in a mess. Martha had given up on him and was about to file for divorce. One night at the Brasseur I had watched them eat dinner together when they inadvertently blundered into the same press camp at the same time. They hardly spoke. Hemingway just sat there, glowering, until Martha finally left the table and went to her room upstairs.

At the same time, Hemingway was deeply involved with Mary Welsh of *Life* Magazine, back in Paris. Although she was to become his fourth wife, she still wasn't divorced and there

49

were stories that Hemingway had shot holes through a picture of Mary's husband in her bathroom. He must have been torn to pieces emotionally that summer and fall, and it showed when my path crossed his, both in Paris and Luxembourg. Though he was only forty-five years old, he looked sixty. His already enormous bulk was swelling to the dimensions of a Hungarian wrestler; his graying walrus moustache and habitual two-or-three-day's growth of stubble could not hide the pouches on his bloated face; he complained constantly about his hair falling out and blamed it on his helmet, which he frequently refused to wear, even under heavy artillery bombardment.

He knew that I had worked for *Collier's* too, and treated me with a certain amount of deference, although he told others that I was a bit too cautious and over-worried about saving my ass. He called me—not entirely without affection—"kid" or "punk."

When I opened the door to Schloss Hemingstein, there was a tremendous amount of activity going on inside, but my eyes were able to fix themselves only on the central figure of the bacchanalian tableau. Hemingway, his huge body encased in a white fleece-lined coat, was sitting in the middle of the room in a high-backed wooden chair that looked like a throne. He was drinking wine from one bottle, crudely hand-labeled "Schloss Hemingstein," and urinating into another.

"Hello, punk," he said.

7

I can't remember too clearly what happened after that. There were about eight GI's in the room—playing touch football as I recall, using an empty wine bottle as the ball. The game stopped when Hemingway greeted me, and someone shoved a full tumbler of cognac into my hand. He apparently had drawn it from an immense jug of Courvoisier—the biggest I'd ever seen—standing about three feet high on the floor alongside Hemingway's chair. As soon as I had drunk the cognac, an uncontrollable weariness came over me, which was not surprising since I had been up and driving now for about forty-eight hours without sleep.

As I began to fade, I noticed that the room was filled with clumps of soldiers, the floor all but paved with wine and cognac bottles. I'd never seen so many bottles in my life—not even in a bar.

A couple of the GI's had picked up the children and taken them over to Hemingway. He held each child in turn on his lap. With a display of tenderness that surprised the hell out of me, he chucked Freddie under the chin and Lisa on the bottom. Then, as if through a tunnel, I heard Hemingway roar out orders that the children be given fresh milk from the cow in the barn and put to bed in the featherbed upstairs. I don't recall his ever getting up out of the chair.

The next thing I knew I was on the floor some place and someone was trying to install me in a sleeping bag. It tickled, and I began to laugh in a silly way. Finally I decided to cooperate with whoever it was trying to pull the sleeping bag up around me. A door closed, and it was dark. But under and around the door flowed the strains of an accordion and a banjo playing, New Orleans style, "When the Saints Go Marching In."

The music seemed to recede in the distance, and I was out.

When I awoke, I was totally disoriented. I didn't know where I was, and I thought I had gone to sleep on the ground somewhere. I had a moment of panic at the thought of Lisa and Freddie, but then I remembered our arrival at Schloss Hemingstein and that someone had fed them and put them to sleep. With that recollection, I relaxed and tried to pull my aching head together.

There was faint light outside the window, and I groaned. I thought I had just dozed off for a few minutes and that it was the dawn coming up. But then I looked at my watch and realized I had slept nearly twelve hours. It was dusk, not dawn.

As my senses began to work, my nose picked up an extremely gamy odor surrounding me. In time, I realized that the odor was emanating from *me*. I remembered then that my last bath had been at Giselle's, and speculated on when I'd have my next one.

After that, my ears began to function. They picked up the sound of continuous artillery fire. It didn't seem to be close.

Finally, my eyes returned to duty. They were able to elevate themselves from floor level and to inform my brain that I was in the downstairs bedroom of a typical Belgian farmhouse built of stone. The interior walls were rough plaster, peeling away from the stones in several places. There was a huge, dark wood armoire in one corner and no other furniture except for a high bed. Army overcoats had been hung over the one window for blackout purposes, but they had been carelessly placed and I could see the Brussels lace curtains, beautifully worked by hand, hanging in the window behind the coats. The delicate white did not go well with the dirty olive green.

With my brain now being properly serviced by my senses, I wondered if this was the same Schloss Hemingstein that Hemingway had occupied earlier. Combat artist John Groth had told me that when he was involved with Hemingway's Irregulars and sycophantic AWOL's back in September, the farmhouse from which the novelist held forth was outside the border town of Buchet—almost due east of St. Vith. Since I was reasonably sure I had passed through one of the armored columns on the St. Vith road and had driven well to the south of it, I figured I now must be in or near the Grand Duchy of Luxembourg. Thus, I decided, Hemingway must have returned from Paris, established a new Schloss Hemingstein, and attracted a new set of sycophantic AWOL's.

Not that I cared. All I wanted to do was gather up my two children and deposit them with the Fourth Division. I figured that on the basis of Hemingway's past operations, he must have some contact with his buddies in the Fourth, and that they must be just off our flank somewhere.

I was wrong—but it took me a couple of hours to find out.

I struggled out of the sleeping bag and walked into the main room of the farmhouse to find the children. The scene that greeted me was like something out of a Roman Polanski movie of twenty-five years later.

There were soldiers in various degrees of undress, wearing the shoulder patches—when I could see them—of the 4th, 28th, 99th, and 106th Divisions. One rangy character wore a Michigan State sweatshirt over his Army tunic. Two GI's were playing chess, except that they were jumping the pieces over each other in some strange form of checkers. One soldier was strumming a wild flamenco tune on a mandolin. Another was standing on his head in a yoga position. Yet another was emptying cans of C-ration and bottles of champagne into a cauldron on the red-hot iron stove.

The room was filled with smoke and the fumes of booze. Hemingway still sat in the high-backed chair, a bottle on his lap. His massive head rested on his chest, and I thought he was asleep. But then I realized he was looking down through his steel-rimmed spectacles at a scrap of paper and reciting, to a couple of GI's, the words of a poem he had written. It was something about "that old whore, Death." It suddenly occurred to me that the kids and I were the only people in the room who were sober—and I wasn't too sure about the kids.

Freddie and Lisa were playing happily in a corner. Lisa had acquired a doll, and one of the GI's was talking to her in halting German. Freddie was blowing up a condom, as if it were a balloon. One of these drunken clowns must have given it to him and taught him to tie a knot in it to keep the air inside. I had seen hundreds of French and Belgian kids doing the same thing with rubbers given to them as a gag by GI's, but now, for some reason, I got pissed off. I jerked the blown-up condom out of Freddie's hands and tossed it into the middle of the floor; two of the GI's started playing soccer with it. Freddie gave me a baleful look, and then came over and clutched my thigh. Lisa left her doll—I guessed it was one of the farm children's—and clutched my other thigh. They seemed glad to see me. I didn't quite know how to express affection to children so I patted them on their heads and went outside to the privy.

I relieved myself and tried for some personal sanitation with half-frozen water I found in a cattle trough. It was still biting cold, and a damp mist still hung over the countryside. My jeep was the only vehicle in the farmyard. I looked inside the barn, which was part of the same slate-roofed building as the living quarters. There were a cow, a horse, an old wagon, and a couple of bicycles. I thought of the tattered doll Lisa had found and wondered what had happened to the farmer and his family. I also wondered how this motley troupe of AWOL's was going to get out of here when the Krauts came, which—judging by the intensifying sound of the artillery fire—wouldn't be too far in the future.

I sloughed back to the main room of the farmhouse. Lisa and Freddie were now occupied with some cutouts which must have come from the same child's toy-cache in which Lisa had discovered the doll.

Hemingway looked up from his poetry muttering and said, "Fill your belly, kid." The cauldron on the stove was steaming by now and I used a canteen cup to dip out a batch of the wretched-looking mess. It didn't taste too bad, though. This was the first hot meal I had eaten in two days, and I was ravenous. The children had been up for a long time and had been fed—one of the GI's assured me—but they came over to sit with me and had some of the champagne stew too. I made a mental note that a good vintage champagne can make even C-ration meat palatable, and that if I survived to own a dog in civilian life I would feed the combination to the beast on his birthdays.

While I ate, Hemingway was organizing his "irregulars." He pointed to the yoga practitioner and to the two chess-checker players and said, "You, you, and you. Go out on patrol. If you see any Krauts, fire off this flare-gun." I wondered how any of us could *see* a flare, what with the mist and the overcoats over the windows, but I refrained from comment. The patrol went dutifully outside, first filling their canteens with cognac from the monstrous demijohn of Courvoisier.

Once they'd gone, Hemingway glowered at me. "How did you latch on to these Kraut kids?"

I explained, as briefly as possible. He nodded gravely, as if this were the most natural occurrence in the world. He mumbled, "Jews, huh?" I held my breath for a minute, but he simply let his head fall on his chest and said, "Nice kids. Hope they make it."

Lisa must have sensed something because she came over and clutched my thigh again.

"Listen, Ernest," I said, "I know you're having fun and games here, but the Krauts have broken through all around us and if we don't pull out—"

He interrupted me with a coughing chuckle. "You and those other chicken-shit correspondents," he said, "you must have had a ball when I was called on the carpet down there at Third Army."

"I only heard the rumors. I didn't pay any attention to them one way or another. Now, about hauling-ass out of here—"

He interrupted me again. "Yeah, those cocksuckers really tried to rack me up. You know who got my ass in that jam? It was some chicken-shit rear-echelon correspondents, probably your buddies. That's who. They tried to make me out a horse's ass and a show-off. Those miserable sons-of-bitches, I can out-shoot and out-drink and out-fuck any one of them any time of the day."

I was curious now about how he had escaped the rather serious charges that he had illegally acted as a combatant at Rambouillet and elsewhere, and I asked him what happened.

"What *happened?*" he bellowed. "I'm a writer, and I'm better at making things up with words than any of those chicken-shit bastards. *That's* what happened." The bellow changed to a guffaw at the recollection. "Some of your reporter friends had told them I threw away my correspondent's patch and that I had said I wasn't going to file stories any more. I told the Inspector General's Board I had taken off the tunic with the correspondent's patch because it stank in the August heat and I didn't want to wear it until I got it washed. When they said I was called Colonel and was commanding troops, I explained that it was an honorary title, like General in the Chinese Army. When they asked me about the weapons in my room, I told them I was just storing them there for my friends, the guerrillas.

When they asked me about giving orders to the FFI and going out on patrol with them, I said I was just gathering material for my stories and acting as an interpreter for the American liaison officer, Major Thornton. I got the bastards so confused they let me off. That's what you get for fucking around with a guy who knows how to write fiction."

He snorted and helped himself to some brandy. I didn't know what to say so I just stood there. Both children were now clutching my coat, apparently upset by what they must have thought was an argument.

Hemingway looked up at me through his glasses. "You don't like me, do you, kid?"

I felt stupid about how to answer that, and it showed. "I really don't know you too well, Ernest."

"No, I know you don't like me. All you young bastards are the same. You read my books in college and then when you see me doing the same thing I've been doing almost since before you were born, you think I'm a horse's ass. Goddamit, that's the way I *work*. I see what's true and I take part in it, and then I put it on paper and it's a story." He turned his head slightly to transfix me with a stare. "I'm only talking to you like this," he said, "because I've read your stuff. Some of it is shit but some of it's O.K. You wrote shit when you covered the hedgerow fighting in Normandy because you weren't out there in the blood and the puke yourself. You put down on paper what other guys told you. On the other hand, that story you did about the shine artillery outfit was good. It was true. You were with them in their holes, and you listened to what they were saying. That was great when they slammed the shells into the breech of the 155's and said, 'Rommel, count your men.' And then, after they fired the 155's, 'Rommel, how many men you got now?'"

I was childishly flattered that the Great Man had read my work. But remembering the genuine heroics of the all-Negro

57

333rd Artillery Battalion, I must have blanched when Hemingway used the word "shine" and a deep-south field-hand accent.

Hemingway noticed it.

"And that's another thing with all you goddamned young New Deal liberals," he said. "Every time I use the word 'shine' or 'kike,' you get outraged. I'm from a different generation, goddamit. I was brought up calling Jack Johnson a shine, and Louis Brandeis a kike, and Enrico Caruso a wop, but so did everyone else in those days. That didn't mean I admired those men any less for being able to do something better than almost anyone else in the world." He gulped another drink and muttered, "Everyone's getting so goddam sensitive."

He turned to me again and said, "Tell me, kid, do you think what I'm writing for *Collier's* is shit?"

In line with Hemingway's dedication to what was true, I fumbled for at least a half-truth. "I think," I said, "that it's a little bit shit."

"Wrong," he roared. "It's all shit. But you can't understand that either. I'm used to standing at a desk and polishing each sentence maybe a hundred times, but here I have to lock myself in a hotel room and turn out that drivel for *Collier's* once every month. Here, the goddamned Army won't let me go out and participate and feel, which is the only way I know how to capture what's true. You, with your goddam reporter's tricks, know all the shortcuts. But I can't do it, Saroyan can't do it, Irwin Shaw can't do it, *no* goddamned novelist can do it. *This* fucking war is too big, it's too much. The Spanish war was better. It was manageable."

Just then, a series of incoming shells passed overhead with their familiar freight-train roar. A moment later we could hear other shells exploding in the woods somewhere to our left. The children began to cry. The GI's in the room stared vacantly.

Hemingway's expression didn't change. "Tell me, kid," he said, "are you afraid of death?"

"Goddam right I'm afraid of death," I said. "Aren't you?"

"No," he said, almost sadly and with a kind of shyness. "I'm afraid of some day not being able to get it up anymore. And I'm afraid of some day not being able to hunt and fish and sail anymore—which I guess is what men do as an excuse for not having to prove to themselves they still can get it up. And I'm *always* afraid of not being able to write anymore.

"But no, I'm not afraid of death. I sat in a goddamned house in the Hurtgen Forest, and two Kraut shells came right through one wall and out the other. Everyone else was cowering in the cellar, but I just sat there, not giving a shit if the shells exploded or not. Do you know how my father died? He blew his head off with a rifle. I never understood him too much, but I admired him for that act of courage. When the time came when he was sick and felt inadequate, he brought on his own death gracefully. Grace in death is like the *coup de grace* in bullfighting. It doesn't require the interaction of still another person to inflict it."

More shells came over.

"Ernest," I said, trying to comfort the trembling children, "I'm tired of listening to this goddamned bullshit. Now where's the goddamned Fourth Division?"

"I don't know," he said, and took another belt from the bottle. "I just stopped off here on my way from Paris to Luxembourg."

8

That cut it for me. I gathered up the children and buttoned them carefully into their coats. Familiar by now with Lisa's bathroom proclivities, I took the kids outside to the privy and then deposited them in the jeep. I scouted around until I found the well—it was the hand-pump kind—and filled my canteen and a jerry-can with water.

When I got back to load the jerry-can into the back of the jeep, the GI's—about fourteen of them—were standing around the farmyard in confusion, listening to the shells bursting in the distance. I ignored them, having encountered in previous attempts at conversation only the silly giggles and self-conscious bragging of too-far-gone inexperienced drinkers. They still were giggling and carrying on among themselves. Using my flashlight in the semi-darkness (a little light was coming from the ill-covered windows of the house), I checked my other jerry-can and noted that I only had enough gasoline for forty-five miles or so.

As I climbed into the jeep to take off, one of the GI's stepped up to speak with me. I recognized him as the one who had been talking with Lisa in German. He was a skinny kid with dark-rimmed eyeglasses and a helmet that seemed at least two sizes too large for him. He couldn't have been more than nineteen. He wore the patch of the 106th.

"You a sergeant?" he asked.

"Yes, how did you know?"

"Colonel Hemingway told us."

This one, at least, seemed to have sobered up some.

"Do you guys know who Colonel Hemingway really is?"

"Some of us do, some don't. I read one of his books in school back in Milwaukee—the one about the guy and the nurse in Italy in World War I."

Since I had been thinking of the motley group as genuine sycophants, this piqued my curiosity. "How did you ass-holes get here in the first place?"

"Running," he said. "We saw the lights and came in and started eating the food and drinking the booze."

"How did you personally get here?"

"My outfit was up there in the line near Cavender. I was only with them two days. A month ago I was going to college in Colorado in the ASTP program. They yanked me out, gave me a couple of weeks of basic training, and then sent me over here as a replacement. I ended up in this rifle company in the 106th. I didn't even know the other guys' names when it happened." He shuddered. "It was terrible."

I was losing patience. "What happened?" I demanded.

"The first night it was quiet. It was almost like a ski resort, one of the guys said. The second night, all of a sudden there were shells and mortars falling all around us, and the Germans were coming out of the mist in white coats so we could hardly see them. My platoon leader told us to fall back to a fence line and dig in. We dug our holes and were waiting there, and an hour later the Krauts in the white coats were coming across the field again. Then there was a German tank behind us. The tank just went up and down our holes, firing its machine gun into them. God, it was methodical. They couldn't hit one guy in his hole so the tank just stopped over the hole and kept running its engine—to kill the guy with the fumes, I guess. When I saw that, I got out of *my* hole and took off for the woods.

Everybody else who was still alive was doing the same thing. I didn't stop running until I saw the lights and I came here."

The boy was crying now. I didn't know what to do to stop him. He said, "You're a sergeant. Get us out of here."

I marveled at the ability of the Army to inculcate men with a blind faith in command in a little more than two weeks. But in my three years of military service I had never ˙ssued an order to a single soldier. The only time I thought of myself as a staff sergeant was when I typed the rank on phony sets of travel orders I made up for myself.

But I pondered the choices the GI had raised for me. The kids and I in the jeep, with enough food and water for the three of us, would have a fairly good chance of sneaking through the lines unobserved. On the other hand, if we did run into trouble, it might be better to have a squad who could draw off the fire and maybe do a little fighting themselves—when they sobered up. Besides, I now felt sorry for them.

Time to sound like a sergeant. "All right, you ass-holes, fall *in!*" They formed a scraggly weaving line.

"How many of you guys got rifles?"

Only three of the fourteen held up their hands.

"How many of you guys ever shot a rifle in combat?"

No hands.

"How many of you guys know how to read a map?"

No hands.

I thought, "What a bunch of eight-balls"—but then I remembered *I* didn't know how to do any of those things either.

I thought for a moment and said, "O.K., any two of you who were brought up on a farm, hitch up the horse to the wagon in the barn. Six more ride in the back of the wagon. Two of you ride the bicycles that are in the barn. The rest walk. You all fall in behind me, and I lead the way in the jeep. Except you." I pointed to the boy who spoke German. "You ride with me in the back of the jeep. I have a special job for you."

The GI's scurried around in the courtyard, and in about five minutes they surprised me by having the horse and wagon, the bicycles, and themselves all lined up behind the jeep. Lisa and Freddie were chattering and looking up at me with admiration. They seemed to be thrilled with the way I was barking orders—and having them obeyed—in such a fine military fashion. Freddie, in fact, kept imitating me, saying things like "Fall in!" and "All right, you guys."

We were just about to pull out when the door of the farmhouse was flung open and the vast bulk of Hemingway stood silhouetted against the light. "Wait for me, you silly sons-of-bitches," he yelled, "I'm coming with you."

He climbed into the farm wagon, settled in a corner vacated for him by the six GI's already there, and fell fast asleep.

Our bizarre caravan wound its way down the back-country lane. I had to limit my speed to five miles an hour so the horse could keep up. The horse, nervous over the artillery fire and the mandolin music one of the idiots persisted in playing, kept snorting and shying. One of the farm boys finally got on the animal's back and worked the reins from there. That seemed to quiet the horse down. Behind the wagon, the two bicyclists and the men walking were strung out for about a hundred feet.

We had moved along for half a mile in this gypsy fashion when the boy in the back of the jeep spoke up: "Sarge, what was that special job you had for me?"

"Oh, yes," I said, "I want you to teach me German."

"*What?*" he said. "The whole *language? Here?*"

"No, you ass-hole," I replied. "Just a few of the basic words, like 'ear' and 'nose,' so I can communicate with these kids. Where'd you learn your German, anyway?"

"At home, in Milwaukee. Almost everybody in Milwaukee with German parents speaks some German. But I'm afraid I don't remember too much, and my parents' dialect is *Plattdeutsch* rather than *Hochdeutsch*."

"Fuck the dialect," I said in my sergeant's voice, "just teach me some words."

So for the next two miles I was a student. *Mund,* I learned, means mouth, *Badezimmer* means bathroom, *essen* means eat, *Kleider* means clothes, *laufen* means run, *vorsichig* means careful. I already knew that *Liebchen* means sweetheart.

The children thought this was a great game. I had told the boy to instruct them to whisper, as we were, and with each word they gaily clapped their mittened hands and whispered in unison, *Mund* means *mouf, Kleider* means *cloves, Badezimmer* means *boffroom.* I counted the lesson a striking success when Lisa informed me that she had to "go boffroom." Then I realized that the instruction had taken an entirely unexpected turn: she had learned the English more readily than I had learned the German. This gave me an idea, and I began to try French words, on the chance that the children might have picked up some of that tongue, too, during their brief stay in Spa. "*Méchant,*" I said. "*Schlecht,*" they said, clapping their hands. "Bad," I said. "*Méchant* is *schlecht* is bad," they said.

"Well," I said, "with a little mixture of French, German, and English, I think we're going to get along just fine."

They didn't understand *that,* but just then I discovered that I had something more serious to worry about.

We had climbed a slight hill, and suddenly the mist ahead of us was glowing red and yellow. The boy in the back of the jeep said, "Looks like there's a hell of a fire down there, Sarge."

Hemingway didn't hear or notice. He was asleep.

I stopped the caravan and appointed a two-man patrol to scout ahead on foot, the Milwaukee youth and a plump kid who seemed to be coming out of his cups.

I waited anxiously while they crept down the road. They were back in fifteen minutes. There was a village at a crossroads ahead, they reported, and the whole goddamned town was burning. Obviously it had been hit as a specific target by the Kraut shells we'd heard going overhead back at the farmhouse. The Krauts could have thought it was an assembly point for our troops.

"Anyone in the village?" I asked.

"No," they said. "The civilians must have cleared out. No Krauts there, either."

I cranked up the caravan and we pushed forward cautiously. My scouts were right. The village, lifeless, was a mess. The stone houses had partly caved into themselves and onto the road. Whatever was left inside the buildings was burning fiercely. Smoke and dust hung in the mist like a giant multiplication of Los Angeles smog. The only building that didn't seem to have been touched by the bombardment was a tiny gas station on the edge of town.

There was a single hand-operated pump out in front. From experience, I knew the pump would be dry—and it was. It had been a long time since gasoline rations had been issued to civilians. But knowing the Belgian and Luxembourgeois character, I was aware of the fact that you could find some interesting things behind a legal façade. I was right. In the rear of the building were two drums of black-market gasoline, probably from U.S. Army stores. And through the window I could see an elderly Citroën taxicab, standing there in splendid solitary majesty. I decided to investigate the taxi after I had filled the jeep's tank and the jerry-can. The cab seemed poised for a quick getaway, but obviously its owner had not been able to get back to it from the blazing village.

I had just about finished with the jerry-can when I heard the taxi's motor cough and growl. Looking out the dusty window I saw Hemingway, squeezed in behind the wheel. He revved the Citroën's engine a couple of times and then took off in a spew of snow and mud, thundering away in the direction of the village crossroads like a besotted Thor.

I was sorry to see him go, and glad to see that he had regained his style. But then again, he somehow didn't belong with our ragtag band blundering its way along in the backwash of battle.

Now, should he be killed, he would at least go out with the grace he so admired. (Actually, as I learned later, he arrived, terribly sick, at Fourth Division Headquarters in Rodenbourg on December 20. He spent two days in bed, being treated with sulfa drugs, and in a little more than a month he was on his way back to his home in Cuba, via London and New York.)

As I watched the Citroën disappear in the winter mist in that little Belgian or Luxembourgeois village (I still don't know which), I fleetingly regretted my noncommital answer when its driver had said, "You don't like me, do you, kid?"

9

I think Hemingway took the crossroads to the south. Because I heard artillery fire in that direction, and also to the north, I led my collection of eight-balls straight ahead. The road was so serpentine that I soon had no idea which direction our caravan was taking; a few quick looks at my compass semi-convinced me it was more or less westerly. If so, I had completely reversed course from the one I'd set out on from Spa two interminable days before—when I had turned east toward Eupen.

At this point, I didn't care. All I knew was that we seemed to be in a corridor between two separate conflicts and that, as long as I could, I wanted to avoid crossing an armored convoy —or a battle area—with fourteen eight-balls and a horse. So long as it was quiet ahead, that's the direction I'd keep going in.

My troops, after a period of nervous reflection, up to and including our passage through the burning village, were getting restive. I suspected they had brought some of the cognac bottles along with them and were replenishing their loads. There were occasional raucous outbursts behind me, and twice I had to stop and tell them to shut up. The second time I made them line up and took a head count. Two of the GI's who had been marching on foot were missing. After questioning the others,

I figured that the dropouts were simple victims of alcoholic exhaustion, sleeping off their loads in the woods somewhere.

I was down to twelve eight-balls.

We kept going for about two hours. We crossed two empty paved highways, but my previous experience told me to stick to the country lanes—and we did. One of the lanes seemed to run parallel to a highway for a while, and we suddenly heard a peculiar clatter from the road, a hundred yards or so away. Our horse neighed. There was an answering chorus of neighs from the road.

The farm boy riding our horse slipped down from his mount and came running over to the jeep. "Sarge, does the Army of the U.S. of A. have cavalry over heah?"

I listened to the clatter and the neighs and said, "For Christ's sake, the Krauts must even be using horse-drawn artillery in this offensive."

We crouched down in the woods, but we couldn't make the horse crouch—or even stop neighing. I was sure the Krauts would send a patrol, if only to pick up another spare horse. But gradually the clatter subsided and it was quiet again in the woods. Except for Freddie. *He* was making neighing sounds now in an apparent attempt to provoke our horse into a response. A few words from my new German vocabulary, *"Halte den Mund,"* shut him up.

An hour before midnight we came to a village. We had passed many hamlets before whose houses were all dark and shuttered, but here was a building with light blazing from two of its front windows. There was a sign proclaiming the establishment to be the Café des Deux Soeurs. Seeing the lights, I enjoyed a moment of exultation, thinking that maybe we had outrun the war. But the still-reverberating sound of the big guns quickly doused that hope.

I stopped our little convoy and sent the Milwaukee boy on foot to see if any Kraut vehicles were parked behind the café.

70

Certainly there were none in front. He came back and said there were no vehicles of any kind—Kraut, U.S., or civilian.

I decided to go into the café so that we could at least find out where we were. I never got to ask the question.

As I approached the front door, it opened on its own and a woman stood there, smiling and bowing obsequiously, and saying "welcome" in German and French, *"Willkommen, bienvenu."* I noticed immediately that she didn't say it in English. She wore a nipped-waist, bouffant-skirted black dress that was right out of a Betty Grable movie and her muddy blond hair was pinned up in multiple braids. She looked about thirty-five.

I glanced past her into the room. There was a well-lit bar, and four other women sitting around languidly in Betty Grable dresses. One of them wore a turban, which made me remember, vaguely, that the Belgian *Armée Blanche*—the underground—had shaved the heads of women who had collaborated with the Nazi occupation forces. My suspicion was confirmed when I saw a battle banner of the 1st SS Panzer Division newly hung—or just replaced—behind the bar.

The woman in the door apparently was confused by my conglomerate correspondent's uniform, but she had no trouble identifying that of my farm-boy jockey who had sauntered up behind me and was gaping into the café.

"Why it's a 'ho-house," he said delightedly. "Them's 'ho's in theah."

The woman's face turned black. *"Américains!"* she spat out, and slammed the door.

By now the rest of my squad had gathered around—attracted, no doubt, by the farm boy's dancing up and down and shouting, "It's a 'ho-house, a 'ho-house." They assembled outside the door and began beating on it.

The door opened again, and I saw that a startling transformation had come over the lady in Betty Grable black. She apparently had had a quick consultation with her colleagues:

her sour face now beamed with a dazzling smile. *"Entrez,"* she said, "welcome." With a great cheer, my entire Army surged inside. The lady deftly avoided their charge and then reappeared in the doorway.

"Vous parlez français, monsieur?" she asked. Now her voice was throaty, like Edith Piaf's. Before, it had been reedy.

"Oui."

A Gallic shrug: she must have noticed my reaction to the German battle flag. *"Les affaires sont les affaires,"* she said. I also just shrugged.

"Entrez, mon choux," she coaxed. *"Vouz êtes très gentil."*

Her musky perfume was beginning to get to me. It was wafting all over me, propelled by the warm air from the room behind her. I followed her inside. She smiled a knowing smile. The musk-and-perfume was overpowering now. The room was filled with giggles and rebel yells; the heat from the open fireplace began to melt all the cold and stiffness I had endured over the past two days. The lady in Betty Grable black glided off to fetch me a calvados. I unbuttoned my coat and began to extricate myself from it.

Just then I remembered Freddie and Lisa waiting in the jeep outside.

I was tempted for a moment to bring the children in and pay one of the girls double, just to take care of them for an hour or so.

Instead I went over to the Milwaukee boy, who was nuzzling an enormous blond's half-exposed breast. I put on my sergeant's voice and said, "Hey, Mac, go out in the jeep and sit with the kids for a while until I come out."

"Fuck you," he said, not even looking up.

Everyone else seemed to be locked in for the rest of the night, so I buttoned up my trench coat again and went out to the jeep to try and figure out another solution.

Both of the children were crying. Lisa grabbed my coat and wept huge tears all over it. She was calling me "Papa."

I knew then I was hooked. I also came to my senses and realized that this was a terribly dangerous place to stay—a natural checkpoint for any Kraut patrol wandering by.

I quieted the children with K-ration chocolate and tucked them in warmly in the front seat of the jeep. I started the motor and headed west again along the road.

As we left the village, heavy white flakes began to fall. If it didn't let up, I guessed at least a foot of snow would be on the ground before morning.

I heard the lonely neigh of the horse behind us. It was a pretty good old horse. I hoped the farm boy would remember to feed it some time during the night.

PART II
Fubar

December 20-23, 1944

10

Tarfu (Things Are *Really* Fucked Up) had escalated to Fubar (Fucked Up Beyond All Recognition).

It stopped snowing, but the thickest fog in fifty years had settled all over the Ardennes.

The overwhelmingly superior Allied air forces had been mostly grounded for four days. On the few occasions when they ventured out, more likely than not they bombed American-held towns and positions through the fog.

Twelve hundred German paratroopers, under Colonel Friedrich August Baron von der Heydte, had left Germany in 105 big Junkers troop-carrier planes. Their objective: to drop five miles north of Malmédy and disrupt the American rear. By mistake, two hundred of the paratroopers descended on Bonn, deep inside the Reich. Only twenty-six had landed successfully with Baron von der Heydte, and now they were wandering and hiding in the Belgian back country—like me.

SS Lieutenant Colonel Jochen Peiper had taken his elite 5,000-man tank task force through La Gleize and into Stoumont, but there he ran into the U.S. 30th Division and part of the 3rd Armored. Peiper was out of gasoline, and other German units were trying to float cans of fuel down the river to him from Stavelot. Peiper was trapped. He had advanced less than a dozen miles from the site of the Malmédy Massacre.

The 2nd Panzer Division, on the other hand, had smashed through Clervaux and crossed the Ourthe River at Ourtheville, using a massive American Bailey-bridge that our engineers failed to blow in time because one of them wet the dynamite fuse by dropping it momentarily in the river. The 2nd Panzer had gone all the way to Celles, three miles from the Meuse River in the middle of Belgium, and more than thirty miles ahead of any other German unit.

On the north shoulder of the Bulge, the U.S. 1st, 2nd, and 9th Infantry Divisions were holding fast on Elsenborn Ridge, a high point of land used since medieval times by the Belgians, and the Dukes of Liège before them, to repel invasions from the east.

On the south shoulder of the Bulge, the hapless Volksgrenadier divisions—the ass-holes of Von Rundstedt's army—couldn't make a dent in the U.S. 4th Division and the 9th Armored Division around Echternach, on the Luxembourg-German frontier.

General George Patton had wheeled his U.S. Third Army and was joining the battle on the south flank.

In between the north and south flanks of the Bulge, everything was confusion. Three full-sized German armies were milling around over a forty square-mile area, but their forward onrush toward the Meuse and the North Sea was impeded by an American peninsula (the St. Vith sector) and by an American island (Bastogne), both jutting into their lines. Both would have to be reduced before Von Rundstedt could resume the main thrust of his pocket *blitzkrieg*.

I didn't know all of this, of course, on the morning of December 20, 1944. But I was able to piece a lot of it together as Lisa, Freddie, and I huddled in a forester's cabin in the woods. I learned what I could from interpreting the lies issuing from both sides over my little portable radio. That is, until its batteries faded and gave out at about 11 A.M.

The children and I had spent most of the night groping our way first through the heavy snow and then the dense fog. In a way, the lack of visibility was a blessing. Several times we could hear men and machines within a hundred yards or so of us, but we never saw them. Each time, I stopped to determine whether the voices were American or German. They were always German. Twice I took to the woods to circumnavigate what I was sure were roadblocks. In those after-midnight hours, the artillery fire was sporadic, and I heard no small-arms fire at all. You couldn't hit what you couldn't see. In the swirling fog, thicker than anything I had experienced in London, the Krauts didn't seem to be bothering to send out patrols.

I had even become bold enough, after a while, to drive with my headlights on—they could reach only about ten feet into the fog, anyway. I was lucky to do five miles an hour, but occasionally, when the headlights allowed me to follow well-defined shrubbery in the snow alongside a road, I was able to get up to ten miles an hour.

We had left the whorehouse at 11:30 P.M. At 4 A.M. I glanced down at my odometer: we had traveled exactly twenty-eight miles. We were on a narrow dirt road in what seemed to be an extremely thick fir forest. This forest wasn't anything like the scientifically planted ones we had negotiated further east. It was for real: huge firs, naturally spaced, with deciduous trees growing at random among them. The forest floor was not a neat carpet of needles but a thick tangle of underbrush. I saw a snow-covered track leading off through the underbrush and decided we had gone far enough for the night. I kept urging the jeep along the track for about two miles until it became little more than a footpath and the underbrush stopped me completely.

I was ready to bed us down for the night in the snow alongside the jeep, when I flicked on my flashlight—and there, just a dozen feet away, was the deserted forester's hut.

The kids and I were so exhausted that we could hardly

make it inside. It was cold but dry in the hut. I had brought my Fortnum and Mason sleeping bag with us, and also an Army blanket.

I sighed, tucked the kids into the sleeping bag, and wrapped myself in the blanket on the dirt floor beside them. We all must have been asleep in thirty seconds.

When I awakened, my watch told me it was 9 A.M., but the heavy fog outside still made it nearly pitch-black in the cabin. I went out to the jeep and got some K-rations, a small gasoline-operated primus stove, and the radio. When I got back, the kids were up and already playing with the tattered doll and the cutouts they had taken with them from Schloss Hemingstein. Lisa wanted to eat just the chocolate from the K-ration breakfast package, but I made her swallow some of the dreadful ham-and-egg combination in the little cans, which I had heated on the primus stove. Freddie ate everything with no urging.

The stove now had made the hut quite comfortable, and we settled in for the day. Our only course was to rest until nightfall and travel under cover of darkness.

While the children amused themselves with what seemed to be a silly word game in German, I listened to the radio. From time to time, Lisa came over, leaned on my upthrust knee, and gazed at me coquettishly. Freddie became very interested in the radio, especially when I was tuned to the German stations. When the batteries finally went, I gave the radio to Freddie to play with. That was a mistake. He obviously was mechanically inclined, and in no time at all he had the components all over the floor. I called myself a *schmuck*—it was at least possible that I might find more batteries the way I had found the gasoline. But Freddie was so childishly intent on the tubes and condensers that I didn't have the heart to bawl him out. Lisa was busy again with her doll.

I took advantage of their involvement with their own interests to work on my notebooks. I still wasn't sure we were going to get out of this alive; but, I reasoned, a reporter should at least go out with a few words scribbled down for whatever posterity there might be. I never had developed the facility of total recall, which some writers have, but in my civilian days I had learned to listen to an interviewee with apparent disinterest—to throw him off guard—and then rush to the men's room to make my notes while everything was fresh in my mind. The war, with its constant interruptions of shells and bullets, had forced me to sharpen this technique even more. So now I put down everything I could remember about the flight from Spa: Chick, the whorehouse incident—and especially that remarkable session with Hemingway.

I finished with the notebooks at about 1 P.M. All this time, not a sound had penetrated the dense woods—not even artillery fire. We dined on a canned Danish ham I had been saving in the *Lootwagen,* and then I settled down again with my Michelin Atlas to try to figure out where we had been during the night and where we were now.

I got a cold chill as I traced our apparent course. If the Hemingway farmhouse had been toward the north of Luxembourg, and if my compass had been correct as I traveled due west, we must have passed—in last night's impenetrable fog—just north of the Kraut perimeter building up for the assault on Bastogne, which is almost all they were talking about in the news on the radio.

After the shock of that realization wore off (I had a daytime nightmare fantasy about our having passed through a whole Nazi division in the dark) I continued to draw a line on the map, running due west from the area just above Bastogne. The line ran into a great empty section, marked on the map with wavy blue lines. Only two roads penetrated the blue-line void, which extended for several miles south and west of the Belgian town of Barrière de Champlon, about halfway between Luxembourg and the Meuse River. The blue-line void was labeled *Forêt de Freyr.*

We must be in the Great Freyr Forest.

I went to the door, opened it, and looked out. I could see nothing but the huge firs, the mantles of snow weighing their lower branches nearly to the ground. It reminded me of the forest in the Canadian Laurentians when you travel the dirt roads far beyond the ski resorts.

I began to feel safe for the first time since taking that lonely highway to Spa. I wondered who could ever find us in here. Why couldn't we hole up in the hut until the battle was over? I couldn't believe that with Montgomery and Patton applying pressure from the north and the south, the Krauts wouldn't be pushed back eventually.

At the same time, I had a feeling that this was the same kind of false-security exultation experienced by the shipwreck victims in novels.

I decided to enjoy the exultation while it lasted. I turned back into the cabin and resolved to face something I had been nervous about since morning.

I put on my sergeant's voice and barked, "All right, you guys. Hop to it. *Baden, baden.* Bath time."

The children watched with mingled wonder and trepidation as I got a GI towel, a Dorchester Hotel washcloth, and a bar of George V Hotel soap out of the *Lootwagen.* I then filled my helmet with snow and placed it on the primus stove. When the snow had melted, the helmet was only a quarter full, so I went outside with the kids and showed them how to make snowballs to add to the now hot water in the helmet. *"Knoedel,"* (dumplings) trilled Lisa, clapping her hands after dropping her snowballs into the helmet.

When there was enough hot water, I decided to get the toughest part of it over first. With mock solemnity I bowed to Lisa and said, *"Fräulein?"* She bowed back, puzzlement all over her little face. "O.K.," I said, "off mit der clothes." She hesitated for a moment, then obediently unbuttoned her coat and her dress. Freddie laughed and Lisa made a face at him. When she was finished, flannel drawers included, I told her to hold my trench coat over her like a tent—to ward off as many of the drafts as possible.

She stood there, unabashedly naked. The tiny perfection of her body—matchstick legs and all—made my eyes sting. I had seen a lot of ladies without their clothes on—even including a sneaked glimpse of my mother when I was a curious kid of Freddie's age. But I'd never seen a little girl stripped before. My two sisters had shared a second-floor bedroom while I had commandeered the attic room of our house. And try as I might, I never caught my sisters off guard against the alien in the attic.

With a pang, I thought then of the ladies at the Café of the Two Sisters. Once, *they* had been six years old and innocent and hairless, too.

My helmet with the warm water was on the floor near Lisa's feet. I dunked the liberated Dorchester Hotel washcloth into it, slathered it with the precious soap, and vigorously scrubbed her shoulders, arms, and back. I even washed her chest, feeling under my hand the delicate bones of her ribs. We made a little educational game out of it. I'd say, *"Bras,* arm," and she'd laugh and say, *"Arm."* It was the same word in German, which seemed to delight her. I'd say, *"Cou,* neck," and she'd say *"Nacken."*

I squatted down and picked up each small, pink-heeled foot, and while I concentrated on getting the soap between the toes, her two hands rested on my shoulders. We stayed nose-to-nose in this position for some time, while I groped in my mind for a way to tell her to wash the rest of herself, herself.

"Macht der rest, *bitte,"* I finally said, handing her the cloth. She giggled and did it, my voluminous trench coat still draped incongruously over her spare shoulders. Then we dried her off with the towel, and she put her clothes back on with feminine meticulousness.

Now it was Freddie's turn. He was a lot easier—and even better at the word game. He knew the English words for the parts of the body even before I said them in French. I was disconcerted, though, when I noticed he was developing a bad rash around the crotch: I sprinkled sulfa powder from my first-aid kit on the rash and made a mental note to keep an eye on it to make sure it didn't get worse. I hated to have him put back on his ragged and now dirty underpants, but I didn't think we were set up for laundry-and-drying in the hut at that moment.

I used what was left of the warm water to launder myself slightly—while the kids watched solemnly. I stripped only to the waist. I hadn't reached the point yet where I wouldn't feel funny about letting them see me naked. I wondered what I'd do if I ever had to face that problem with my own kids in my then uncertain future.

Freddie had to go outside to the bathroom, but I made him wait until he had stopped shivering after his bath. I humored him along during the waiting period by promising him he could use the Throne. His eyes glowed with anticipation of this honor and he waited patiently. When the shivering had stopped, I said, "Go, *Mensch.*" He scooted out the door.

In about two seconds he was back, his face white.

He stuttered at me in frightened French, German, and English.

"*Der* jeep," he said. "*Deux hommes* is there. *Einer* is a *deutscher Soldat.*"

11

A German soldier.

I looked around the hut for any sort of weapon. But there wasn't anything there—not even a log I could use as a club.

Then I heard a voice from outside the door. The words weren't German. They were Antwerp-accented French, but ominous nevertheless: *"Sortez! Les mains élevés."*

I came out as I was told, my hands over my head. The children came, too, clutching fearfully at my trench coat.

There was a German soldier there, all right, but he was standing dejectedly in front of another man who was covering both him and us with a Sten gun. The man was medium-sized and bearded and he wore the same sort of fleece-lined coat Hemingway had had. Below the hem of the coat I could see tan-colored military-type pants, tucked into paratrooper boots. On his head was a black beret with a V-shaped silver insignia pinned to it. On his sleeve was a red, yellow, and blue armband. In the middle of the yellow stripe in the armband were the letters "AB."

In addition to the wicked-looking Sten gun, the man was armed with a rifle slung over his shoulder. It was a Mauser, so apparently it was the Kraut's rifle. The Kraut was pudgy, pasty-faced, and wore rimless eyeglasses. I judged him to be in his late thirties or early forties. The shoulder patch on his gray uniform identified him as a member of the 26th Volksgrenadier Division. The Kraut, by his demeanor, unquestionably was a prisoner of the man with the Sten gun, whose armband I recognized as that of the *Armée Blanche*—the White Army, also known as the Belgian Forces of the Interior, and, as in France, the *maquis*.

I smiled with relief. The *maquisard* did not smile back.

I pointed to my shoulder patch and said, "Journalist. *Correspondent de guerre.*"

The man said, "I speak English. German, too, for that matter. Throw over your identification papers."

I tossed him my green-covered SHAEF accreditation folder.

He glanced at it, studied my face in the photograph, and said, "Where did you acquire that jeep?"

I was getting pissed off now. "It's mine."

He said, "Where did you acquire those children?"

I said, "They're mine."

"Do not make jokes with me, monsieur. You may be who you say you are, but there are many Boches in the countryside masquerading as Americans." He pointed the Sten gun menacingly.

I said, "O.K., I'll prove it to you. I spent many weeks with the *Armée Blanche*. Do you know the lieutenant, André Cornet, in Charleroi?" He nodded, and said, "But that means nothing. If you are a Boche spy, you might very well know the name of one of our most famous heroes of the underground."

"All right, then, were *you* in Charleroi when the *Armée Blanche* liberated it from the Boche in August?"

He nodded again.

"Well, I was there for the Battle of the Bridge, and I was there, with Cornet, for the Battle of the Slaughterhouse. Do you remember how the *maquisards* then said that the blood of the

Boche was now mixing with the blood of the pigs on the slaughterhouse floor?"

He was wavering.

I said, "And then came the trial of the two Belgian Waffen SS men we had captured. It was in a room in a chateau, and there were blue tiles on the floors and flowers in the wallpaper. The magistrate, a Monsieur Grammont, I believe, found them guilty. He pronounced them traitors, but since they were wearing the uniform of the Boche, he regretfully had to give them over to the Americans as prisoners of war. The magistrate ripped off their SS collar insignia and gave me one as a souvenir." I fished the little silver double-lightning emblem out of my pocket and threw it over to the *maquisard*.

He lowered the Sten gun. "I, too, was there," he mumbled wearily. He nudged the Kraut with his boot. "Let us now go into the hut and warm ourselves."

His name was Jacques. We drank cognac, and I gave him the last of the canned Danish ham; and he told me what he was doing there. His *Armée Blanche* unit operated out of the *Forêt de Freyr*, and he had been sent out to capture a German for interrogation as to the enemy's intentions in the Great Forest area. He had nabbed the Kraut at an ammunition dump about five miles out of the forest. It had been an easy capture, since the Kraut was supposed to be standing guard duty but had fallen asleep at his post.

Jacques spat some cognac in the direction of the Kraut, who was sitting docilely on the floor in a corner of the hut, munching a slice of ham Lisa had brought over to him. "That pig is a Belgian," Jacques said. "From Eupen, on the border, where they never gave up considering themselves Boches. He says he was drafted into the Boche army. If he had been wearing the black uniform of the Waffen SS, I would have known he was a volunteer and I would have killed him on the spot with this." He pointed to the trench knife in his belt.

The children seemed to be intensely interested in the Kraut. They prudently kept a few feet away from him, but stared at him with mixed fear and wonder in their brown eyes. The Kraut began to speak to them, tentatively, in German. I heard him ask the children their names, and I gathered that he was telling Freddie that he had a son named Friedrich, too.

I didn't listen beyond that because I was absorbed in what Jacques was saying. He said the Great Freyr Forest had been a guerrilla stronghold for years. It wasn't cultivated for trees, like most of the Ardennes, because it had been the private hunting preserve of the Flemish Counts of Freyr since medieval times. I asked him if these were the same Freyrs whose magnificent chateau, facing a spectacular rock-fall on the Meuse River, I once had visited. He said, "Yes, and their ownership of this forest dates back, I think, to the Spanish occupation of the Lowlands, when Charles the First gave it to them." He wrinkled his nose with proletarian scorn. "They used it, for the most part, to hunt wild boar."

I commented that Jacques seemed to have a pretty good grasp of Belgian history. "I should have," he said. "I taught history in the schools in Ghent before the war. I also taught English, French, and German to Flemish-speaking children, which was much more difficult, I can assure you."

This answered the question in my mind about the excellent quality of his English, but it also piqued my curiosity about his presence in the *Forêt de Freyr,* many miles and a cultural eternity from cosmospolitan Ghent, with its university and museums.

"I was coming to that," he said, with a schoolteacher's natural impatience toward a backward student. "When the Boche invaded us in 1940, I was mobilized with my regiment. We were sent to Liège, but before we got there the conquest of our little country already was over." He added proudly, "You may not know it, but unlike the French, our Army never surrendered. Instead, while the Boches were concerned with the British at Dunkirk, my platoon—with several others—fell back on the *Forêt de Freyr,* as our ancestors had done for centuries during previous occupations."

He couldn't resist getting in another crack at the French. "Unlike our colleagues to the south, we retained our military organization. We had the same officers who commanded us in the Belgian Army, and we operated with strict discipline. The RAF dropped weapons to us, and also uniforms and radios. Our orders came from Belgian Army Headquarters in London. We successfully disrupted the Boche's supply lines throughout the Occupation, and—except for the main road from St. Hubert to Barrière de Champlon, which he used with only the greatest caution—the Boche never was able to penetrate the Great Forest. It was an island of resistance he could not conquer."

He paused. "What happened *after* Liberation, you know. We poured out of the Great Forest and joined the battle for Charleroi."

"And then?"

"I went back to Ghent and found only my father and my younger sister alive. I was just about to resume my teaching activities when the Boche broke through again—in the Ardennes. My unit was ordered back into the *Forêt de Freyr.* Our orders are to deny the forest to the Boche, as we had done before, and to harass them from the rear as they attack your American garrison in Bastogne."

I thought about that for a minute and then I asked something that had been percolating in my mind for a long time. By now, of course, I had told Jacques about the children and how I had acquired them. "Is it possible," I said, "that the children and I might join your unit here in the forest until this is over?"

He shook his head. "Unfortunately, no. We have been ordered not to do that, even with our own children. Our effectiveness depends on our flexibility and our mobility."

I grasped at another straw. "Do you have an American liaison officer with your unit?"

"Unfortunately, no. A Major Roberts was dispatched to join us, but we have learned he was wounded as he passed through Manhay. Perhaps another will come by parachute when the fog lifts."

"Is it safe for us to stay here, then, until the new liaison officer arrives and can assist us?"

Again he said, "Unfortunately, no." It was an expression he used a lot. He gestured toward the Kraut sitting on the floor. "That pig there," he said, "has informed me that his company is on its way to dig in on the edge of the forest, just east of here. We will attack them, and you will be in the line of fire. You will have to leave."

"Where to?"

"I will draw you a map. There is another forester's cabin deeper in the woods. There are only rough trails extending that far, but I believe your jeep will be able to negotiate them."

The Kraut had stopped talking with the children now and was listening intently to us. I didn't believe he could understand what we were saying, but apparently he did. He turned to Jacques and spoke to him in heavily German-accented French. "I beg of you, monsieur," he said, "I am a schoolteacher, too." He began to weep. The children stared at him with astonishment, then worry. Despite the gray uniform which had terrified them at first, they seemed to like him.

Jacques peered down at his prisoner with disgust. He did not deign to reply to him in French. He growled something in German, which I took to mean, "Schoolteacher or not, I don't give a shit what you have to say."

"What will happen to him?" I asked.

90

He shrugged. "He will be tried by our military tribunal. It is up to them."

"Will he be shot?"

"Perhaps."

"But they didn't shoot the two Waffen SS in Charleroi."

"That was Charleroi. This is the *Forêt de Freyr.*"

"But goddamit," I said, "Can't you at least listen to what the poor bastard has to say?"

"Poor bastard," said Jacques. "And you with two Jewish children here? Let's hear what he has to say about what happened to their father and mother."

The Kraut, still crying, was appealing to *me* now in his accented French: "But, monsieur, I have nothing against Jews. I have nothing against anyone. I have two children at home the same age as these. Please, monsieur. I am not as brave as you. The *allemands* came in 1940 and they spoke the same language as we Eupen Belgians did, and all I wanted was to be left alone with my family. They left me alone, and I kept teaching in the school. They conscripted me only in October. What could I do? I have been in the field for a week now, and I have not been able to bring myself to shoot anyone. Look at my rifle. Please look at my rifle. It was issued to me after my training was completed, and it still has not been fired."

"Merde de taureau," said Jacques. In any language that meant bullshit. But the *maquisard* did pick up the Mauser and peer down its barrel. I noticed that the cosmoline grease in which the weapon had been packed still had not been wiped from the gunsight. Jacques did not tell me what he saw inside the barrel, but I suspect it was more cosmoline. He looked thoughtful.

"At least this man will be heard before the military tribunal?" I asked.

"Yes," Jacques said. "He will be heard."

He turned away from the Kraut, who had quieted down now, and busied himself drawing a crude map of the *Forêt de*

Freyr on a page of my notebook. He marked in the trails I should follow and the two main roads and the one secondary road I should avoid. He told me that if the battle abated, I could reach Dinant, on the Meuse River, in less than two hours after I emerged from the western edge of the Great Forest. "There are many British troops in Dinant," he said. "They have come down from Montgomery's army in Holland to block the river crossings."

Jacques shook hands with me and said he might see me again. He picked up each of the children and kissed them on both cheeks.

Then he walked out, prodding his prisoner with the Sten gun. In less than five seconds they both had disappeared in the fog.

12

The incident involving Jacques and the Kraut had a profound effect on me. While the children watched, somewhat subdued, I scribbled my thoughts in my notebook.

Looking at these notes many years later, I saw the troubled and muddled feelings of a young man already convinced of the ridiculousness of war. They were not unlike the feelings of another generation, in another time: Vietnam.

The confusing factor for me, in 1944, was Hitler and Nazism, twin monsters that had to be obliterated. In those now faded scribblings I find: "Obliterated, yes. But at what unknown cost? Are we creating our own monsters, who, now that the wine of militarism has titillated their taste buds, will want to continue to fight wars of repression in the name of patriotism? How simple it is to tell the good guys from the bad guys in a Van Johnson war movie. But not here in this little hut. Jacques, the schoolteacher, has become an overbearing prick, and I wonder what will happen if he ever is turned loose on the natives in the Belgian African colonies. The Kraut, also a schoolteacher, only wants to be left alone and not be made to kill other human beings. He cannot bring himself to fire his weapon. He probably will die. Are there millions of others on both sides who march along, and try to survive, and do not fire their weapons—and who die?"

I remember referring to these notes during the Korean War, when I wrote an important article with the U.S. Army historian, Brigadier General S. L. A. Marshall, entitled, "Why Half Our Combat Soldiers Fail To Shoot." * General Marshall and I discovered, through exhaustive interviews, that no matter how great the danger to themselves, *more than 50 per cent* of American troops in the field never actually fired their weapons at the enemy. They had been raised with the Judeo-Christian concept of morality, one of the principal tenets of which is "Thou shalt not kill." It was the despair of the Army that it could not knock these civilian ideas out of reluctant civilian soldiers' heads.

Philosophizing and note-taking completed, I made ready to leave the forester's hut with Lisa and Freddie. It was still daylight, about 3 P.M., but Jacques had warned me I'd never find the trails on his map after dark.

But, as was my habit, I got lost anyway.

Some of the trails, hacked through the woods to accommodate huntsmen on horseback, were too narrow for the jeep, so I had to find detours. On one of the detours we stirred up a nest of wild boars, one of whom charged the radiator of the jeep—to the terror and then the delight of the children. After the beast turned tail and disappeared into the woods, Lisa and Freddie vexed me by oinking and grunting for at least half an hour.

Occasionally a trail became a twin-rutted track. I couldn't see the ruts through the foot-deep snow, but I could feel them under my wheels. Obviously, small vehicles had been here before. Not too recently, though. Every once in a while there would be a fallen tree across the track and I'd have to push it out of the way with the four-wheel traction of the jeep. I let Freddie get out of the jeep to help me remove some of the

* Editor's note: The article won a journalism prize for the best magazine reporting of 1953.

94

smaller trees by hand. He wasn't much help, but I let him think so.

By nightfall I didn't know where I was. The giant firs, once protective, now seemed more immense and more foreboding. The beautiful white-against-green no longer projected a cheery Christmas-card kind of grandeur. It seemed endless; smothering and claustrophobic. I decided we'd better stop for the night— right there.

It was to be our first night in the field, without shelter.

The fog had lifted slightly and was replaced by a biting wind which made pipe-organ sounds as it filtered through the million tiny reeds of the fir needles. Wanting more cover against the wind, I dug a snow trench under the jeep, which would also provide us with some sort of roof in case it snowed again. I piled fir boughs against the sides of the jeep to try to keep the ground winds out. After we dined on cold K-ration, I put the children in the sleeping bag and slid the whole package into the snow trench under the jeep. I wrapped myself in my blanket and got into the trench beside them.

None of this helped. The children were shivering and kept crying. I felt as if I genuinely were freezing to death. Even through my heavy combat boots, I could feel my feet turning numb. Also, the frozen ruts in the road were rock-hard against my back and thighs. It didn't console me much to realize that soldiers in the field were sleeping like this every night.

But the thought gave me an idea. When I'd been with the 1st Division earlier that month, I'd heard an old sergeant talking about a trick he had learned when he was stationed in Alaska. He had said to the men in his squad, "Every time you guys get a copy of *Stars and Stripes*, stick it in your pack when you finish reading it. You're not going to keep it to wipe your ass. You're going to keep it to line the insides of your shoes and your clothes when you're out there in your fuckin' holes and the temperature gets down near zero. A few layers of newspaper is the best fuckin' insulation there is."

So I got out from under the jeep and found a batch of month-old *Yank*'s and *Stars and Stripes* I had held onto for some reason or another. I wrapped the kids' feet in newspaper and put their shoes back on. I wrapped the papers around their legs and under their coats. I did the same for myself. Then we all got into the sleeping bag, with the blanket folded double on top of it.

It was crowded inside the bag. I lay on my back and there was just room enough for Freddie to squeeze in beside me. I held Lisa in my arms as she stretched out on my stomach with her head resting on my chest. The road ruts in my back didn't feel any softer, but at least our mutual body warmth and the layers of newspaper made the intense cold bearable.

With my arms wrapped around her, Lisa stopped crying and fell asleep at what I judged to be eleven o'clock. An hour later Freddie had stopped whimpering, and from his regular breathing I guessed that he too was asleep.

I didn't sleep at all.

By about 3 A.M., my arms and legs were so cramped I didn't think I'd ever be able to use them again. Also, I had to urinate something fierce. I stood it as long as I could, but then I had to get out of the sleeping bag and take care of my needs. That, of course, woke the children up. They never were able to get back to sleep. So we just lay there, shivering. To keep their minds off their misery, I sang to them; but even the ribald verses of the British war chanty, "Bless 'em All," did not distract them.

I gave up at first light. The coming of dawn seemed to revive the children. We all got out of the sleeping bag. I stood around stamping my feet, and the children, watching my every move, did the same. I checked for frozen limbs and frostbite, but except for a little white spot on Freddie's nose, everything seemed to be all right.

Actually, it wasn't as cold as it had been. The wind was gone, and the fog had dropped down again.

I heated up some K-ration breakfast on the primus stove and thawed out my canteen so we could drink water with a little dried lemon powder added. We cleared away the boughs from around the jeep and I tried to start the engine. It wouldn't start. Something had frozen up during the night.

I was about to put the lighted primus stove under the hood—an admittedly dangerous procedure—when I remembered another old soldier's trick. I peed on the carburetor and the battery. The children were enthralled with this procedure and Freddie insisted on peeing on the engine, too. He accomplished it by standing on a fender while I held him by the waist. Lisa sulked, but this was no time to explain her anatomic disadvantages to her.

On the second try the jeep started. We moved ahead up the trail, and in less than an hour we could see the cabin through the trees. It seemed to be built of logs and mud. The only problem was that the road was blocked by a huge fallen fir and there was no way to get around it.

I was numb with fatigue by now, but there was only one thing to do. I pulled the jeep into the woods for a few feet and covered it with boughs. Then I loaded myself down with the sleeping bag, the stove, food, and other necessities, and we climbed over the fallen fir. Lisa tore her stockings and skinned her knee as she came over the log. I couldn't help her because both of my arms were loaded with comestibles. She didn't cry much, though, and I ordered Freddie to give her a hand.

The cabin was only about fifty yards from the fallen tree, but it was all uphill and the snow was deep. It seemed to take hours to get there. When we did, the cabin looked more luxurious to me than my last room at the Dorchester. It had a wooden floor and two windows, and I figured it probably was a gamekeeper's overnight shelter rather than a forester's hut. There was even a porcelain stove, with firewood piled neatly beside it. I started to build a fire in the stove until I remembered that fire makes smoke and smoke curling up from the woods could bring Kraut artillery shells down on us. The Kraut 155's had a range of ten miles or more and were extremely accurate.

So I lit the little gasoline primus stove instead, and we all made ready to put in some long-delayed sack-time.

Before I let myself down into sleep, I worried vaguely about something I had sensed the minute we entered the cabin.

I don't know whether it was the can opener or the heel prints I had noticed on the floor, but the cabin showed signs of very recent habitation.

I just closed my eyes. I didn't want to think about that— or anything else—at this point of delicious semi-consciousness.

Anyway, it probably was Jacques' men.

13

It was Jacques who woke us up the next morning.

He shouted, identifying himself, as he came up the path to the cabin. He came in with two other *maquisards,* both in the same tan paratroopers' uniform and both considerably younger than he. One of the boys was carrying an old-fashioned galvanized two-liter milk can. "We thought you could use this," Jacques explained. "Louis, here, is a local boy. His father has a farm on the other side of the forest."

I poured the milk into my canteen cup. It was fresh and thick with cream, and the children gulped it down. I used some of the milk to scramble some fairly palatable dry powdered eggs from my own stores. We all ate the eggs. They seemed to be a special treat for the *maquisards.*

As we breakfasted, I noticed that the two younger guerrillas were treating Jacques with a certain amount of deference. I asked Jacques, "Say, what rank do you hold in the *Armée Blanche?*"

"Lieutenant," he said. "I'm a platoon commander."

"Then what were you doing out there alone yesterday pulling in a prisoner?"

"That is my specialty," he answered drily. "I do it perhaps better than anyone else."

"Was your prisoner's information accurate about his company digging in on the edge of the woods?"

"It was."

"And what happened?"

"During the night, they were eliminated. For Volksgrenadiers, mortars are sufficient."

"And your prisoner? Did he get good points for giving you reliable information?"

His English wasn't that colloquial. "Pardon?" he asked.

"Is your prisoner still—"

"Yes, he's still alive. He's being dealt with."

"By the military tribunal?"

"Yes."

He wouldn't elaborate, so I changed the subject. "What's going on in the war?"

"Chaos. There are Boches to the north, east, and west of us. But also there are Americans to the north, east, and west of us. When the fog lifts, perhaps the military situation, too, will clarify itself."

"You mean, when our air forces can fly?"

"Exactly."

"What do the weather reports say on the radio?"

"A so-called Russian High is approaching us from the steppes. It is a cool dry air mass that will sweep the fog away."

"When will it arrive?"

He shrugged. "Who knows. Perhaps tomorrow, perhaps Saturday. Perhaps not until Christmas, on Monday."

He seemed moody and not particularly anxious for conversation, so we stood for a few minutes and watched the interesting byplay that was going on between my two children and Jacques' (Louis and the other boy, Christophe, couldn't have been older than sixteen or seventeen, despite their adult-looking ammunition belts and Sten guns).

They sniffed each other out cautiously for a while, like two sets of puppies, and then Louis said to Christofe, in French,

"She looks like my little sister, Françoise." Lisa said in her mixture of French-German-English, "I do *not* look like your little sister, Françoise." She slapped Louis playfully on the thigh. That started it. Soon they were gaily chasing each other all over the cabin in a four-way game of tag. At one point I heard Lisa say, "Louis, *vous êtes un* pain in der ass," and I had to admonish her again about her language.

None of this seemed to amuse Jacques. What a strange man, I thought. He was watching the youngsters with his piercing brown ascetic-looking eyes, but the look in the eyes told me that the mind controlling them was focused on something else, perhaps miles and years away. He had opened his fleece-lined coat. I noticed that in the form-fitting outlines of his jump-suit, he had the build of an all-around athlete—like the decathlon men of my track days in college. He was, in fact, a striking-looking character, with his deep-brown academician's beard and the athlete's body. One thing bothered me about him, though. He kept his right hand in the pocket of his coat and toyed incessantly with something there. The constantly moving fingers made the pocket squirm, as if he had imprisoned a squirrel in it. I somehow couldn't feel comfortable with a man who kept a hand in his pocket while I was talking to him.

I had to talk to him because there were a few more pertinent questions I needed answers to.

"I found a can opener and some comparatively fresh heel marks when we entered the cabin last night," I told him. "How recently have your men been in here?"

"Not since before the liberation in August."

But he didn't seem to be anywhere near as concerned about the phenomenon as I was. "Do not worry," he told me. "The Great Forest is soaking up stragglers the way a sponge soaks up particles in water. If anyone was here in the cabin, it probably was GI's. We do not permit the Boche stragglers to get this far."

That reassured me, but only slightly. I asked him what he

had meant the day before when he said there were a lot of Boches behind the lines masquerading as Americans.

He said, "Skorzeny's men." He didn't have to tell me who Skorzeny was. SS Lieutenant Colonel Otto Skorzeny, one of Hitler's Nordic favorites, commanded a daredevil unit of elite SS paratroopers. Among their other exploits, Skorzeny's men, led by their giant blond commander, had jumped onto a mountaintop in the Alps a year before and rescued Benito Mussolini from his Italian captors.

"What are Skorzeny's men doing here?" I asked.

"They infiltrated the American lines during the breakthrough," he said. "No one knows whether they jumped or just drove. But now they have American vehicles and they are wearing American uniforms. They all speak colloquial American English. They are destroying road signs and blowing up bridges and communications lines. We heard by radio from our liaison at SHAEF this morning that their principal objective is to steal into Paris and assassinate Eisenhower. The General is practically a prisoner in his headquarters in Versailles. He has a company of troops guarding him day and night."

I whistled. "Have you picked up any of Skorzeny's men here in the Great Forest?"

"No," he replied, "but the Americans have established roadblocks to intercept them, all the way from Aachen to Paris." The fingers of his right hand were still working away in his pocket.

The thought of Skorzeny's men depressed me. Despite Jacques' guerrillas, the *Forêt de Freyr* was a perfect place for them to infiltrate—especially in American uniforms. I asked Jacques, "When I leave with the children, where is the nearest American unit?"

He didn't seem terribly interested in our little problem anymore. In fact, his general attitude was beginning to bug my ass again. "The 335th Infantry Regiment is holding a line this side of Rochefort," he said. "About ten kilometers from the western edge of the forest."

So near and yet so far, I thought. Ten kilometers—less than five miles.

Just then, Lisa, being chased around the room by Louis, stumbled over the milk can on the floor. I was sure she was going to land headlong on her face, but Jacques, pulling his right hand out of his pocket, grabbed her just in time to keep her from falling. A metal object dropped out of his right coat pocket as he withdrew the hand. I picked it up.

It was a crucifix.

I stared at the crucifix and gave it back to him. We measured each other for a long moment.

"You mentioned you were a schoolteacher back in Ghent?" I said.

"Yes," he said.

"What kind of school was it?" I asked.

The brown-marble eyes *really* were piercing me now. Then a veil dropped over them, and Jacques shrugged his Gallic shrug.

"*Oui,* monsieur," he said, "I was a priest."

He peremptorily left with his men, and I never saw him again.

14

Even in the comparative comfort and safety of the cabin, I was edgy all that morning of Thursday, December 21. The duality of Father Jacques—and the effect the war had had on him—somehow disturbed me.

I worked on my notebooks for a while, but my heart wasn't in it. I found myself snarling at the constant gloomy fog outside, wishing it would go away. I had the childish thought that if the weather cleared, so would this ridiculous situation.

As I watched Freddie and Lisa, still playing tag in the cabin, I faced what really was bothering me. I had known these children for only four days, and at times I hardly knew myself. My cavalier fuck-the-establishment attitude didn't seem so dashing any more. A week ago, I would have been amused by the Father Jacques incident and categorized him as a rebel, like myself. Now I devoted most of my thoughts to the forces that had changed him—or, maybe, hadn't changed him at all.

It was the children, I decided. They and I together produced some sort of synergistic effect. Maybe it was because for the first time in my life, I was worrying about someone other than myself. I worried about such minor things as Lisa's torn stocking. I worried about the rash on Freddie's crotch, which seemed to be getting worse. He kept scratching it and sometimes whimpering in pain. I told him, *"Nein scratchen."* He corrected my German. *"Kratzen,"* he said.

Perhaps the children were helping me to grow up. But was I ready for this kind of responsibility?

I decided to postpone looking at Freddie's rash until later.

I wandered down to the jeep, the children sliding in the snow behind me, and found a pocket chess set I kept in my pack. I brought it back to the hut. I set it up on the floor and played against myself for a while. It was pretty boring since I knew what moves I had in mind, and Black and White more or less were at a standoff. I wished I had a book of chess problems I could work on.

I noticed Freddie watching me, and then he was squatting on the floor on the other side of the chessboard. Lisa came over and sat beside him. Freddie said, *"Bitte,* papa?" To my amazement, he took the chessmen and set them up properly in their little pegged holes—except that he had the Black Queen and the White Queen on the wrong side of their Kings, a normal mistake. Somewhere along the line someone had taught Freddie to play chess.

We started a game. He didn't play well, but he knew the moves. I tried to throw the game, but his child's impetuosity and short attention span made it impossible for me to lose to him. We set the board up for another game. By now, however, Lisa's attention span was down to zero. She kept tapping me and Freddie on the nose, and finally she uprooted some of the chessmen from their holes in the board. Freddie didn't want to play anymore anyway, so I let it go at that.

The chess episode got me to thinking about the kids' background, and now that we were communicating fairly well in our French-German-English mélange, I sat them down to try and find out what I could about them. They were very vague about their parents. All they could remember was that "mama was *schön,* beautiful." I figured out that they couldn't have been more than two and three when the Gestapo had violently separated their parents from them. The children didn't know their family name. "Westermann," which had been given to me by the woman in Spa, meant nothing to them.

They only could recall a succession of "uncles" and "aunts" —*Onkel Rudolf, Tante Anna,* and so on—and moving in and out of a lot of cellars and garrets. One small boy named Gerhardt seemed to have made quite an impression on them. I gathered from their excited talk about him that they had shared his bedroom at one point. They animatedly described Gerhardt's toys in the minutest detail. I learned all about Gerhardt's gray hobbyhorse with the left eye missing and Gerhardt's train that could whistle as it came through the tunnel.

Wide-eyed as she finished telling me about the train, Lisa said—almost with disbelief—"Gerhardt has a *wirklich,* a *real* papa and mama."

That broke me up and I had to discontinue the conversation. To accomplish this, I announced that bath time had arrived again. It meant checking Freddie's rash, which I had been avoiding, but it was better than trying to interrogate the children further.

The rash was even worse than I had feared. It had concentrated itself into angry red welts dotted with little pus pockets. Freddie winced when I washed the welts and applied the sulfa powder. I examined his ragged and soiled underpants and determined they'd have to go. There was only one solution. I'd have to cut down a pair of my own GI drawers and sew them up again to fit Freddie's minuscule ass.

I found the khaki cotton shorts in my pack and began to attack them with the blade of the Boy Scout knife I carried with me at all times. The children stared curiously at first, but once Lisa realized what I was doing, she acted as if it were the most hilarious thing she had seen in her life. She all but rolled on the floor laughing, and so, after a while, did Freddie.

It got worse as I roughly fitted the cut-down shorts to Freddie's hips and started to sew the fabric back together. All

I had for such emergencies was a single enormous needle, given to me once by Giselle, and some heavy black thread. I made huge cross-stitches with the thread, the only way I knew how to sew. The khaki cloth was soon bisected with rows of half-inch X's, but it began to resemble shorts again—even though one leg was shorter than the other. By now Lisa was curled up on the floor, laughing at me hysterically through her legs. I didn't see what was so funny. I sewed up my own shorts that way.

I finally got the shorts on Freddie, and they seemed to make him feel better. When Lisa subsided, I figured I'd give her some responsibility and assigned her to cook our C-ration lunch on the primus stove. I usually heated the cans directly on the stove, but I let her use my mess kit like a frying pan. She became quite solemn about her responsibility and did a creditable job of the cooking.

Then, because the children slept better in the daytime than at night, I put them down in the sleeping bag for a nap.

I wasn't expecting guests—particularly American guests. But we had them, in about a half hour.

15

It happened this way:

I was outside, stretching my legs, when I heard voices through the fog. They were coming from where I had camouflaged the jeep at the fallen fir tree, about fifty yards away.

One voice said, "Now who could have laid this fuckin' log across the road?"

Another voice said, "Beats the shit outta me, Mac. All I know is we can't move it. It's too fuckin' big."

A third voice said, "Tough titty. You'll just have to move your big fat ass up to the cabin on foot, is all."

A fourth said, "Hey, there's a fuckin' U.S. jeep here under the branches."

I was so overjoyed to hear my native tongue again that I replied in kind. "Hey, that fuckin' jeep is mine," I shouted down the hill. "Leave it alone, you ass-holes."

There was silence for a moment. Then Voice Number One said, "Come down the hill, Mac. Nice and slow. And with your fuckin' hands up."

"With fuckin' pleasure," I said. I practically danced all the way down the hill at the prospect of premature rescue.

When I could see through the fog, there were four soldiers lying behind the fallen tree, three of them with M-1 rifles trained on me. The fourth was wearing an officer's trench coat with a Major's gold oak leaves on the shoulders.

The Major said, "What are you doing in our fuckin' hut?"

I spilled out my story.

The Major looked at me with disbelief. "You got kids up there?" He nodded to one of the GI's. "Search him for weapons, Homer." A tall black sergeant climbed warily from behind the log and frisked me thoroughly. "Nothin'," he said. "He's wearin' a fuckin' war correspondent's patch."

The other two GI's stood up. I now could see they were a T-5 and a Corporal, both white. They went over to the Major and held a whispered conference. They seemed worried.

I thought it strange that three whites and a black would be serving in the same outfit (the Army was years away from integration in 1944) but they all wore the Third Army shoulder patch and I had heard that white and black Quartermaster Corps troops had been organized on an emergency basis to supply Patton's advance across France by truck. They called these elite trucking outfits "the Red Ball Express." On a hunch, I looked beyond the GI's into the fog: two two-and-a-half-ton trucks were lined up on the narrow rutted track behind the fallen tree. It didn't occur to me to wonder how they had gotten there through the woods. All I saw was the red ball painted on the side of each truck. That seemed to explain it. I had read in my own magazine some rather romanticized stories to the effect that the Red Ball Express was capable of anything. At that moment I chose to believe the stories.

The conference broke up. The Major came over to me and asked me for my correspondent's ID card. I showed it to him, and from his expression I guessed that he had recognized my name. "Davidson," he said, "we want to make a deal with you."

"Deal? What kind of a deal? All I want is to get out of here with the kids."

The Major said, "You don't understand. We're not the Army."

I was bewildered, but not too bewildered to notice that he had dropped his "ain't's" and was speaking perfectly good, educated English.

The black sergeant said, "What he means is we separated ourselves from the Army some time ago. It's like we gave the Army a kinda dishonorable discharge."

The other GI's tittered. It was beginning to dawn on me. "You mean you're deserters?"

The Major nodded.

"But what about those two Red Ball trucks back there?"

"We've got a nice little business going," said the Major. "We run civilian merchandise from Marseilles to Paris and Brussels."

"You mean black market?"

"You might call it that. We like to think of it as the free enterprise system in action."

I remembered his opening gambit. "What's the deal?" I asked suspiciously.

"Very simple. We don't want any trouble, and we don't want any publicity. You don't write anything about us, and you don't tell anybody about us. All we want to do is spend the rest of the day here and take off again when it gets dark. When we go, we'll leave enough food for you and the kiddies for a week."

"I take it you've used this cabin before."

"Yes," he said, "it's been a regular way station for us since August."

I said, "Did you leave a can opener the last time you were here?"

"Yes," he said. "Do we have a deal?"

I was surprised that they'd told me what they were up to, and even more surprised that they hadn't just shot me. "Sure," I said. "You have a deal."

The children, though awakened from their naps, were delighted to receive guests. They were very gracious to them. Lisa, already amazingly feminine in her reactions, seemed embarrassed about her torn stocking. She took it off and walked around, harlequin-like, with one black leg and one white one.

The guests, in turn, were gracious to the children. They brought up a whole case of chocolate from one of their trucks, and then began to unload other goodies for a late-afternoon meal. The munificence of their stock made my *Lootwagen* seem like a highway hot-dog stand. They had canned snails from Bordeaux, which they cooked in the shell with olive oil from Sicily and dried chives from Avignon. They had crabmeat chunks, canned in Japan but imported from God-knows-where. They had a magnificent white wine from Burgundy, a Montrachet 1937. They had a canned brandied cake from Italy.

While they cooked this feast and organized the cabin for their rest stop, I had to admire their thoroughgoing professionalism. The chef was Walter, the T-5, and he had a full set of gourmet culinary equipment with him, iron skillets and all. As he puttered about on his own gasoline stove, a type I had never seen before, Homer, the black sergeant, and Marty, the corporal, brought in four eider-down sleeping bags and arranged them on the floor so they did not impinge on the corner the children already occupied. The Major was very much in command of everything. The other men called him Ray.

"Are you really a Major?" I asked Ray.

"Of course not," he said. "I'm a private in the Canadian Army."

"And the others?"

"All privates. In the Army of the United States. Homer *was* a sergeant, though. He got busted for talking back to a white officer. Homer's a welder, one of the best, but he was in Graves Registration."

I wanted to ask more questions, but dinner was ready. It was the best I had had since I had left New York. The children didn't like the snails or the crabmeat, neither of which they had ever seen before. They limited themselves to the chocolate and the heavily brandied cake. The brandy apparently flattened them, what with their lack of a nap, and they both were sleepy before the meal was finished. I put them to bed in their corner of the cabin.

My guests and I then settled down to cigars and after-dinner brandy and conversation.

I was curious about their business, and they were surprisingly frank in discussing it with me. They were as matter-of-fact as garment manufacturers talking about next spring's line of frocks. Following the law of supply and demand, they were buying up scarce luxury merchandise—like nylon stockings—in Marseilles, and selling it at a huge profit in Paris and Brussels. For their return trips, they bought up items that were scarce in Marseilles. It was as simple as that. They had very little competition, since the civilian trucking industry still was nearly non-existent in France after the Occupation.

"But now?" I said. "With one of the biggest battles of the war going on?"

"It's the best time," said Ray. "The fuckin' MP's are so busy trying to catch Kraut paratroopers in American uniforms that all you have to do is give them the right answer when they ask their stupid questions and they let you right through the roadblocks."

"What stupid questions?"

Walter was the one who explained. He was a slight, pimpled boy of about twenty whose gray eyes looked troubled. "Suppose I'm driving one of the trucks," he said. "They stop me at the roadblock and they ask where I'm from. I say 'St. Louis.' Then they say, 'What's the capital of Missouri?' I say, 'Jeff City.' They say, 'O.K., go ahead.' I guess they figure that no matter how much training the Kraut paratroopers had, they wouldn't know *that*."

Homer chuckled. "Another trick of the MP's is to ask about

baseball teams. There's a General, name of Bruce Clarke, of the 7th Armored. They stopped him near St. Vith and asked him what league the Chicago Cubs were in. He said the American League. They locked him up overnight. They say Patton himself had to get him out."

I asked Homer, "But how do you get through the Kraut lines?"

He was older than the others, and the pepper-and-salt stubble on his big coffee-brown face rippled as he laughed again. "We go where they ain't," he said. "Walter, here, is a genius with radio. We got us a field radio that he fixed up so we can hear the Krauts talkin' to each other. So we know where they are, and we go where they ain't. Like here."

"But isn't it tricky just to be running all over the country-side? I mean, deserters—"

Marty broke in. He hadn't said much until now. He was thirtyish and round as a beach ball, with horn-rimmed glasses perched atop an owlish little nose. I had gathered he was the forged-papers and phony-uniform expert. "Not deserters," he said. "AWOL's. There's about a twenty-year difference in the Code of Military Justice."

"All right," I said, "AWOL's."

"There are enough fuckin' AWOL's running around the countryside to man a fuckin' Army Corps," said Ray. "Why, there are nineteen thousand in Paris alone, according to *Stars and Stripes*."

"Is that where you guys met, in Paris?"

Ray obviously was getting a little worried about my reporter's inquisitiveness. "You're not going to write any of this?" he reminded me.

I said, "How about years from now, when the war is long over?"

He thought for a minute and said, "I guess that's all right. By then we'll be straight, and maybe served our time. And besides, you don't know our real names, anyway." He smiled. "I just gotta tell you about the AWOL's of Paris."

He poured himself some brandy and proceeded to do so.

"There are these nineteen thousand guys," he said, "who are fed up with this fuckin' war and the military chicken-shit, and they live like kings in Paris. Some of these guys make themselves five thousand dollars a week stealing Army supplies and selling them to civilians on the black market. They steal gasoline, cigarettes, soap, anything they can get their fuckin' hands on. They highjack trucks, and they walk in and out of the supply depots like they owned them. I know one Major, a real Major, who highjacked a whole fuckin' train. He sent thirty-six thousand dollars home last week alone."

This made my own occasional petty larceny of personal foodstuffs and such seem silly.

"Is that how you guys got started?" I asked.

"Not really," said Ray. "We all went over the hill from our outfits at about the same time, and we met at the *Deux Magots* on the Boulevard St. Germain. We all were mixed up in the gasoline-heisting bit, but we didn't like it. We decided to pool our talents and go legitimate. Well, almost legitimate. All we needed was the two trucks, some uniforms, and the radio. That's the only heist we ever made from the Army."

The conversation veered away from specifics and onto the various forms of chicken-shit that had caused them to go AWOL, chicken-shit being army vernacular for petty, meaningless tyranny by self-important officers and noncoms. Everyone had his own favorite chicken-shit story.

Ray, for example, had gone AWOL from his Canadian outfit in Antwerp after months of harassment by his company commander, who didn't like Americans. It was the first I knew that Ray was an American. "This son-of-a-bitch Captain once went from Windsor across the river to Detroit to buy a Ford, and when the Ford turned out to be a lemon, he got the idea that all Americans were out to screw him. So I got all the shit details. I dug latrines from Torquay to Eindhoven. The last straw came when I just finished carrying the bodies out of the Rex Theater in Antwerp, which was crowded with soldiers when it was hit by a V-2. The cocksucker made me polish my boots at four in the morning because they were covered with blood."

Homer's chicken-shit story was of the more classic variety. He had been in an all-black Graves Registration Company with all-white officers, specifically chosen from the South. Although he was a sergeant, he was called "boy" by his company commander and forced to put in busboy duty in the officers' mess. His big trouble came when ten mattress covers—in which bodies were buried—were found missing from the hundreds in the supply tent. The night before, the company commander had seen Homer with a white Belgian girl. Homer was accused of stealing the mattress covers to provide dress material for his "whore." The next day, after protesting the charge, he was busted from sergeant to buck private. A week later, he took off.

I felt constrained to tell a few chicken-shit stories of my own. The one they seemed to enjoy most was about a fag First Sergeant at 205 East 42nd Street. I described the way he'd hover over our desks while we were writing our *Yank* pieces, and the instant one of us looked up from the typewriter to think for a moment—even in mid-sentence—the First Sergeant would decide he wasn't working and he'd be hauled off to load packing cases.

The black marketeers loved that one.

By late afternoon, Homer, Walter, and Marty were asleep in their sacks. Ray, an admitted insomniac, sat up talking with me for a while.

"So you're an American," I said.

"Yes."

"Midwest?" I had catalogued his accent.

He nodded but didn't say from where.

I said, "The next logical question, I suppose, is what were you doing in the Canadian Army?"

"I went up across the border to Winnipeg and enlisted in

1939," he said. "I couldn't wait for us to get in. I was a fuckin' patriot in those days."

"If you don't mind my asking, did you go to college?"

"I did."

"And what were you doing before you went up to Canada to enlist?"

He glowered at me for a moment and said, "Let's put it this way. I was in a profession allied to yours. Aside from that, mind your own fuckin' business."

Then he softened. "I know what you're thinking," he said, "but it's my way of beating the system, just like you've got your's. We'll be caught, of course, and have to serve time. But for now, it isn't a bad life, and we don't have to put up with the chicken-shit. We're socking a lot of money away, and we live pretty good. In the cities, it's officers' clubs only. Marty makes up the goddamnedest ID cards and travel orders and officers' uniforms."

He yawned.

"Just a couple of more questions," I said. "First of all, how'd you get your trucks in here?"

"Oh, that," he said. "If you go back down the trail, you'll see a scarred tree about a quarter of a mile from here. If you pull aside the bushes under the tree, you'll find a new road through the woods, leading to a trail which leads to the St. Hubert highway. We cut the new road once when we were hauling a tractor in the truck. Use it when you leave. Our compliments."

I marveled at his misplaced ingenuity. "One other thing," I said. "Why didn't you guys just kill me and the kids instead of going through all this?"

"We don't like violence," he said. "Besides, I read you in *Yank,* and I wanted to see what kind of guy you are."

"You read *Yank?*"

"Yeah," he said. "We *deliver* it sometimes."

16

My black-marketeer guests awakened at about 10 P.M. It was later than they had anticipated, but that didn't seem to bother them. Apparently they weren't planning to travel too far that night. They never told me whether they were heading north or south on this particular trip.

All of them had slept well—except for Ray, who said he'd just lain in his sack, eyes open, the whole time. The others had done a lot of snoring, and, as they woke up, a lot of farting. The snoring didn't disturb the children, but the farting did. They got out of their sleeping bag and came over to sit beside me—one head on each knee.

When the men were up, Walter made some coffee. It was Kenyan, I noticed. With it they ate hard British biscuits. They offered me a cup of the coffee, which was delicious. I suddenly realized this was the first *real* coffee I had had in months. Ever since England, it all had been powdered or *ersatz*.

Working with military efficiency, the men then got ready to leave. They took turns lugging the sleeping bags and their other impedimenta down to their trucks, but mostly it was Ray and Homer giving the orders, and Walter and Marty doing the lugging. Peculiar, I thought. The Army was anathema to these men who had totally rejected it, yet it had left an ineradicable imprint on them. Unconsciously they had adopted a typical Army chain-of-command method of operation.

The reason I hadn't slept was that I was still worried about the black marketeers' intentions toward me and the children. I knew Ray had said their policy was to stay out of further trouble by avoiding violence, but they had told me too much, too willingly; as if they knew all the time they could use their M-1's to eliminate us as a source of evidence against them.

My tension eased a bit when I saw that, between trips to the truck, the men were playing with the children. Freddie and Lisa were enchanted by them as they mock-buffeted them about. They especially seemed to like Homer, who, I guessed from the experienced way he handled the kids, probably had children of his own at home. At one point Homer sat on the floor, put one arm around each of my children, and told them the whole story of *Pinocchio* in capsule form. It was all in English, but Lisa and Freddie listened eagerly and gasped and laughed in all the right places. I still don't know how this secret communication with children works, but they seemed to have understood every word.

I began to relax. I couldn't believe that anyone who could tell stories to children would then turn around and shoot them.

I relaxed even more, when, on their last trip from the truck, Walter and Marty brought in two jerry-cans of gasoline and a heavy cardboard carton. They pushed them into a corner and then, on a nod from Ray, they and Homer took off down the hill, first rumpling the children's hair.

Ray stayed behind. My tension returned.

But he simply pointed to the carton and told me what was in it: candy, cookies, "iron cow" (cans of evaporated milk), and tins of meat, fish, and vegetables. "You got a girl friend?" he asked unexpectedly.

"Yes," I said. "In Brussels."

"I also left you three pairs of nylon stockings. They go for ten dollars a pair on the black market in Brussels—when you can get them."

I thanked him, and he went over to the door.

"Stay out of jail, kid," he said, laughing. And he was gone.

The children, obviously disappointed that our fascinating company had departed, were cranky for a while. I calmed them down with a feast of cookies and evaporated milk, mixed with melted snow, from the new stores—and they went back to sleep.

I sat up half the night thinking about the anomaly of Ray and his men. The thinking continued into the morning, when it became light enough, through the continuing fog, to take notes.

As I promised Ray, I never used the notes until now—when it doesn't matter anymore. I actually didn't find out what happened to the little band of black-market entrepreneurs until 1948, and even then the updating came about inadvertently.

I was doing an article for *Collier's* about World War II's most famous AWOL, Pvt. John Martin, who had amassed a small fortune while he was over-the-hill and was one of the organizers of those nineteen thousand AWOL's in Paris. I worked on the story with Sgt. Al Grey of the Army's Criminal Investigation Division.

Since Martin also had skipped from the Canadian Army, I remembered Ray and asked if CID had ever had any dealings with him. Grey asked me to describe him and then said, "Oh, yes, but his name wasn't Ray. We picked him up in Namur around Christmas time in 1944, right smack in the middle of the Battle of the Bulge. He's serving time in Canada. Ten years, I think, but he should be eligible for parole soon."

He paused. "A funny thing," he added. "We busted two other dudes with him, but there was a fourth man in the gang, a colored guy, who got away. Ass-holes like this usually sing on their own mother if they think it'll get them a few years off on their sentence. But not these dudes. Not one of the three ever told us a thing about the colored guy."

In 1948, I had mixed feelings about this news. I knew an officer who sat behind a desk in the same war, who was much respected and much decorated, and whose virtue never was questioned. Yet, using his cloak of legality, he had master-minded—from behind his headquarters desk—the same sort of operation Ray had run.

After the war, this officer was able to buy a two million dollar radio station with his earnings.

Despite the lack of danger, Friday, December 22, 1944, quite possibly was the most depressing day I had since I was handed Lisa and Freddie in Spa. The children were irritable and with no visitors, for a change, I couldn't find anything to divert them. Freddie's rash was getting worse, and several times he cried. The omnipresent fog literally was giving me claus-trophobia. I thought of the endless days ahead and despaired of ever getting out of the gloomy *Forêt de Freyr*.

I tried to snap myself out of it by thinking of how beautiful these same Ardennes must be in the spring. A friend of Giselle's in Brussels had described it beautifully. "You would never know the winter Ardennes from the spring Ardennes. In the spring, the flowers along the roadsides form a frame of color for the patches of the light-green fields and dark-green for-ests. The fences are not fences, they are blossoming vines. Everywhere there is the perfumed smell of new growth. The cows drop their calves and the horses their foals, almost at the same time, and the young animals dot the fields with black-and-white and brown. The ancient ritual of the renewal of life is more beautifully played out in the Ardennes, I think, than anywhere else in the world."

Looking through the window of the cabin at the dull gray-and-green, I wasn't helped much by these poetic thoughts.

Late that afternoon, I did find a diversion for all three of us.

It came about because thinking of Giselle's friend's lyricisms inevitably started me thinking of Giselle. I fantasized a bit about her lissome body and wondered if I'd ever see her again. This train of speculation led to the three pairs of precious nylon hose Ray had left me as a present for her.

At that moment, Lisa came into the cabin from one of her innumerable trips outside to perch on the Throne. Her torn black cotton stocking was now in tatters, and the normally white leg that showed through the gaping holes was an interesting shade of lavender because of the cold. She shivered violently for a few minutes, and I made her stand directly in front of the gasoline stove to thaw out her nearly bare left leg.

It was then that an interesting problem in textile engineering raised itself in my mind. The theory phase occupied me for the better part of an hour. The problem was: Is it possible to convert a size 8 woman's nylon stocking into an item of clothing that would fit a child's six-inch foot and a pipestem twenty-four-inch leg?

I decided that, what the hell, I'd experiment. It only meant blowing one pair of Giselle's stockings, and the chances were I'd never get to give them to my Belgian flower anyway.

Nylon had been invented just before the war, and its quality was infinitely higher than what passes for the stuff in women's panty-hose today. In fact, the reason nylon stockings were almost nonexistent in the United States at the time was because the entire industry had been converted to the manufacture of nearly indestructible cloth for parachutes. A woman who did have a pair or two of nylons treasured them and cared for them like jewelry. They did not run easily, they were incomparably sheer, and, with the proper treatment, they lasted up to a year.

"Come here, *Liebchen*," I said to Lisa.

She reacted suspiciously to the tone of my voice, but she dutifully came over anyway.

We had a communications impasse as I tried to find out from her the mechanical principle whereby she kept her stockings up. From her pre-bath disrobing, I knew that her stockings disappeared somewhere under her flannel underpants, but I was totally ignorant as to what happened to them there. Somehow she had managed to keep that a secret from me with an instinctive feminine cunning. I had seen her bare-ass naked, but her goddam underwear? That was a private matter.

I finally got through to her what I was trying to do. She giggled, blushed, did a timid little dance, and finally showed me the shirt she wore under the top of her dress. The shirt terminated beneath her underpants, and attached to its bottom hem were four cotton tabs, on which were mounted garters. I felt like Archimedes when he discovered the water displacement theory in the bath tub. I knew the engineering problem could be licked.

By now, Freddie too had become fascinated with my project, and the three of us became so involved in it for the rest of the afternoon that we forget our respective ennui's.

First, I slid Lisa's left leg into one of the nylons. It looked ludicrous. The foot was half again too big and the stocking itself was at least a foot too long; in addition to which it hung on her stick-thin leg like a collapsed sail on a mast. The children clapped their hands and howled with glee. I said, "Wait a minute, you little bastards, I'm just getting started." That made them laugh even more.

I took the bottom of the stocking and folded it under Lisa's foot for added warmth, and the foot still slipped easily into her shoe. Next I concerned myself with the top of the stocking. I turned it back so that about twelve inches hung loose, but I was able to hook the folded edge into the garters of her undershirt. I then took the entire mass of hanging nylon and made a knot in it above her knee. It was miraculous. Once the knot was tight enough, the stocking didn't look too good but it stayed there. A full inch of emptiness still existed between the inside of the stocking and Lisa's leg.

I similarly fitted the other leg, and then, heady with my triumph, I decided to explore even newer scientific frontiers. Lisa's worn flannel underpants were something I had fretted about for a long time. They had been washed so often I couldn't understand how they could protect her from a spring zephyr, let alone the frigid Ardennes blasts. So while I was in the mood, I set about attacking *that* problem, too.

I took one of the second pair of Giselle's nylons and cut off the top. I had Lisa step into the severed stocking top with both feet and told her to pull it up to her waist. It fit—with amazing snugness—because, as I had suspected, Lisa's waist was no thicker than the average woman's thigh.

While I tucked and fussed with the nylon top, I sent Freddie to fetch me my enormous needle and heavy black thread. This sent the kids into further gales of laughter as they recalled my sewing efforts with Freddie's miniaturized underpants. I withstood their scorn, however, and set to work with my big black X-shaped stitches, improvising a crotch at one end of the cutoff nylon stocking top. When I finished and slipped on my ingenious creation, she had an imperfect but serviceable pair of fancy drawers to wear as a buttress over her flannel ones.

At that point, Lisa probably was the only six-year-old kid west of Suez with a complete set of nylon lingerie from the navel down.

She did look like a small baggy-pants clown, but she was so delighted that she kept pirouetting around the cabin to show it all off to Freddie's and my masculine eyes.

By the time it was over, we were ready for dinner and bed. We had gotten through a particularly difficult day.

I enjoyed a delicious night's sleep. I was having a wonderful dream in which I ran naked with Giselle through a light-green Ardennes field bordered with flowers and thick with cute little black-and-white newborn calves.

In the dream, Giselle and I were just about to couple magnificently amid a quadrangle of calves when we were suddenly attacked by a giant swarm of bees. We couldn't get away from them. I woke up in a sweat, but the sound of the millions of bees buzzing continued.

As I struggled back to consciousness, I suddenly realized that what I was hearing wasn't bees at all. It was a stream of airplanes passing overhead. I closed my eyes again. No, it's bees. But when I opened them, No, it's airplanes.

I threw off my blanket and rushed to a window. It wasn't gray outside anymore. It was golden. That was real sunlight filtering down through the firs.

The Russian High had arrived.

It was Saturday, December 23.

17

I ran out of the cabin, the children trailing behind me. They were waiting, I suppose, for an explanation of what had gotten me so excited, but I didn't take the time to deliver it. All I wanted was to find out what was going on up there in the skies over the Ardennes on the first clear day since the Battle of the Bulge had begun.

I couldn't see a damned thing. The firs were too tall and too thick.

Spurred on by desperation, I began to explore our immediate area—something I had not been able to do, since the fog had enclosed us in a gray stockade only fifty feet or so in diameter. I realized for the first time that the cabin was perched on the side of a good-sized hill and fairly close to what might be the summit. I reached that deduction because, just above us, I could see an outcropping of rock through the trees and the top of the rock seemed to be higher than the tallest trees. At least I couldn't see the tops of any more trees on the other side of the rock.

I decided that if I could climb to the top of that rock, or escarpment, or whatever it was, I might be high enough to be able to see something of what was going on. I started up the hill toward the rock, and had actually gone about fifty feet before I remembered the children. I turned around to find them looking desolately at me from where they were standing beside the cabin. "Goddam it," I said, and trudged back down to where they were.

I gave them breakfast as quickly as I could because I wanted to get to the rock while the planes were still overhead. I kept one ear cocked on the sound while I cooked some Spam. I didn't bother to eat. While the children munched their food silently, I rummaged in my pack for a pair of high-powered Zeiss binoculars I had taken from the body of a Kraut officer in a cellar in Aachen. I toyed with the idea of taking Freddie with me on the climb up the rock. I knew Lisa couldn't make it—especially in her new nylon finery. But then I figured it would be best for Freddie to stay in the cabin with his sister.

The children stared at me as if I were abandoning them forever. I said, rather sharply, "Goddam it, I'll only be gone a half hour or so, *demi-heure*." I didn't know how to say it in German. I took off up the hill. I didn't turn around, but I knew they were watching me from the window.

When I got to the base of the rock, it was much tougher to climb than I had thought. It rose, almost perpendicularly, about sixty feet from the forest floor. I used up the *demi-heure* just getting to the top. I made it by finding hand holds here and there, grabbing onto young fir seedlings that somehow were growing out of clefts and crevices in what I now knew was a small escarpment.

I was exhausted when I reached the summit. It was sharp as a knife edge and dropped off just as steeply on the other side. But I was above the trees and I could see the sky.

I clung to the knife edge by propping my foot against a dead fir trunk that had not survived its struggle to exist in its crevice. Then I looked up.

It was a sight the like of which I hadn't seen since the entire Eighth and Ninth Air Forces were thrown against St.-Lô to blow that hole in the German lines through which we poured all the way to the Siegfried Line. Here, a steady procession of C-47 transport planes marched across the sky, from west to east. Above them, knots of American and British fighter planes flew their tight V-formations. I didn't see a single Kraut aircraft in the area—not even the unchallengeable jet ME-262.

I whipped out my binoculars and looked off to the east, in the direction of Bastogne. I could just barely make out the C-47's wheeling and dropping supply parachutes. Even through the glasses, the parachutes seemed scarcely bigger than soap bubbles, but I could see they were different colors—red, yellow, and green. The colors, I knew, were to give the ground troops quick identification of the load the parachute was lowering—food, ammunition, medical supplies, or whatever. I never learned the colors, and they kept changing them anyway.

There also was the color black in the lapis-lazuli blue sky. These would be the puffs of exploding shells from the Kraut 88-millimeter anti-aircraft batteries surrounding Bastogne. Occasionally, a puff would come close to one of the C-47's and I'd watch the plane spiral slowly and gracefully downward, like a moth flicked in mid-air with an insecticide spray. Sometimes, then, I'd see white soap bubbles in the sky as the C-47's crewmen bailed out in their parachutes. Sometimes there would be only one or two white soap bubbles. Sometimes none.

After a while, I lowered my binoculars from the sky and saw a cultivated plateau about ten miles from the edge of the Great Forest; and, beyond the plateau, a heavily wooded ridgeline. As I scanned this vista, I suddenly found myself watching a battle. It all seemed as unrealistic as seeing a war movie from the top row of the balcony of a theater, which I had done frequently as a boy, hissing Erich von Stroheim and shouting at Victor McLaglen to "Watch out!" as he stumbled unheedingly into a Heinie ambush. (In that long-forgotten war, they called them Heinies instead of Krauts—at least in the movies.)

Actually, what I saw from the rock could have been a war

comedy—if I hadn't been conscious, from previous experience, of the torn and burning bodies on the ground. My binoculars weren't powerful enough to see them.

The first thing I noticed was an American reconnaissance squadron coming down a poplar-lined road in the middle of the cultivated plateau. They were traveling north to south, rather jauntily and carelessly, at about forty miles an hour. I knew they were a reconnaissance outfit because of their vehicles. They had armored cars, mounting comparatively ineffective 37-millimeter cannon, and peeps fitted with .50 calibre machine guns. Peeps are jeeps. The motorized cavalry, persisting in its quaint individualisms from the horsey past, had to have a special name for everything so they wouldn't be mistaken for plain old dirty infantry.

Anyway, the peeps and armored cars came barreling down the road, and just then I caught a glint of something up on the wooded ridge above them. Training the glasses on the ridge, I saw the unmistakable outlines of Kraut Tiger tanks moving north—in the opposite direction from the recon outfit—along what must have been a tree-hidden road on top of the ridge. With the white stars on the U.S. vehicles and the black crosses on the Kraut tanks it was like the good guys and the bad guys in the movies.

It was then that I wanted to shout "Watch out!" to the good guys. Which would have done as much good as my yelling from the balcony in the theater.

I saw orange muzzle flashes from the ridge, and the second and third vehicles of the American recon column blew up. Each went in a great burst of flame and black smoke. One of them, as I recall, was a truck and had probably been carrying ammunition. The sound of its explosion didn't reach me until seconds later.

Miraculously, the lead vehicle of the American column—an armored car—didn't seem to be touched. It immediately spun around, with its amazingly short turning radius, and took off in the opposite direction at about sixty miles an hour. The other vehicles followed suit, and the whole outfit went tearassing back up the road to the north. The Kraut tanks apparently couldn't maneuver their 88's fast enough, because the shell bursts now were hitting well to the rear of the fleeing Americans.

Just then, a flight of three U.S. Mustangs passing overhead seemed to take note of the situation and lazily banked down to take a look. Having done so, the planes made three strafing runs along the ridge-top road. They used only their machine guns, and I guessed that they'd already dropped their bomb loads elsewhere and were returning to base for more. From my remote point of view, the planes appeared to be awfully casual about the strafing. They'd make a run at tree-top level, then pull up and fool around in the sky for a while before coming back. They didn't seem to be doing much damage to the buttoned-up Kraut tanks, but, of course, I couldn't be sure. At least I didn't see any of the Tigers blow up.

The entire aerial attack took about five minutes, but it stretched out infinitely longer for me. Then I saw the lead Mustang point itself in the direction of the retreating *American* column—I could almost hear the flight commander saying, "Aha, let's get *that* one, just for good measure."

So they strafed the U.S. recon outfit, too.

The armored cars were pretty far away by now, and I couldn't see any casualties. The peeps dispersed in a patch of woods they had reached. The armored cars, like the tanks, probably had closed all hatches and were shedding the machine-gun fire. I could almost hear the cursing that must be going on inside the armored cars and over their radios.

Fascinated at having this extraordinary ringside seat, I stayed up on the rock until my empty stomach told me it was well past lunch time. There wasn't much more to see. The Kraut tank column disappeared from the ridge, and after a while, even the planes stopped flying. All that was left in my immediate range was the remains of the truck and peep, still smoldering on the pretty poplar-lined road. I could hear but not see the artillery at Bastogne, to the east. There also was the sound of guns to the north, probably, I guessed, around La Roche.

I decided I'd better get back to the cabin to see how the children were doing. Now that the excitement was over, I was beginning to worry about them. I had never left them alone for so long a time.

Climbing down was much more difficult than climbing up, and it took me a good forty-five minutes to make it to the cabin.

When I got there, I found a mess. The food cartons had been opened, and cans were strewn all over the floor. My pack had been taken apart, and my underwear and such was draped around the hut. My first instinct was concern for the safety of Freddie and Lisa, but there they were, on the floor, sulking in a corner. I didn't have to ask them who had done the damage.

They reminded me of a Siamese cat I once knew. When left alone at home for any length of time he deemed excessive, he'd take his revenge by pulling all the toilet paper off the roll in the bathroom. Freddie had gone even further. He had removed his new underpants and scratched his rash until it was seeping blood.

The two children sat there looking at me, expecting to be punished. I didn't disappoint them. I gave each of them some healthy whacks on the ass. Then I cleaned up Freddie's rash as best I could. Then I made them straighten up the mess they had made in the cabin. Then I gave them some more whacks on the ass. Then I sent them, crying, to bed without any lunch.

I sat there for a while, eating some cold C-ration, and trying to figure out what to do. In just six days I had spoiled these children badly, and I now realized I just didn't have the experience with kids to know how to handle them properly. As much as I cared for them, I had to get them to someone who did.

Also, Freddie's rash was now so bad that it needed medical attention. I was afraid he might develop a serious infection, or even blood poisoning.

And finally, my ringside seat on the rock had made me both restive and apprehensive about what was going on in the war. With our decidedly superior air forces in operation, the battle obviously was going to turn that very day. On the other hand, the *Forêt de Freyr,* even though known to be held by the Belgian *Armeé Blanche,* could be bombed and strafed at any time—just as the American recon column had. And we were particularly vulnerable, being so close to the top of the highest point of land in the forest.

Having weighed all these considerations, I made my decision. We would leave that night after dark and try to reach the American lines at Rochefort.

I got out my blanket and stretched myself on the floor to get a few hours' sleep as preparation for the long night that lay ahead. At about 4 P.M., Lisa came over to cuddle beside me. She had forgiven me.

Freddie was a little more stubborn. It took him until 4:20 to forgive me.

PART III

Snafu

December 23-27, 1944

18

By that Saturday, December 23, the war's confusion had downgraded itself two full degrees—all the way from Fubar through Tarfu and right back to plain old ordinary Snafu.

To use one of Field Marshal Bernard Montgomery's more exasperating expressions, "the battlefield had been tidied up." On the north flank of the Bulge, he had forged a continuous Allied line of battle-tested U.S. divisions, extending from Elsenborn Ridge nearly to the Meuse River. American General Lawton Collins' Seventh Corps was even then wheeling into position to close the final gap on this upper edge of the German penetration.

To the west, the British Second Army had blocked all the Meuse River crossings to Von Rundstedt's panzers.

On the south flank of the Bulge, General Patton's Third Army had moved into the line from Luxembourg to Bastogne and General Omar Bradley, in command of the southern front, was beginning to apply nutcracker pressure. In Bastogne itself, the beleaguered 101st Airborne Division and other attached troops had been resupplied by air. Brigadier General Anthony McAuliffe already had replied "Nuts!" to the Germans' demands that he surrender, and the siege of the city—which had fatally delayed the Germans—soon was to be lifted.

Oddly enough, so obfuscated is military communication that

some units still were unaware of the fact that the Germans had broken through or even that a major battle was being fought. A squadron of the U.S. Fourth Cavalry Group, for example, was attacking Duren, a few miles beyond Aachen and well inside Germany, when the Panzer Divisions smashed into Belgium and Luxembourg on December 16. The squadron kept advancing toward Duren until they were pulled out and sent westward on the 22nd. The cavalrymen thought they were going into a rest area, and that night, when they reached Ciney in Belgium, near the Meuse River, they went to sleep in a schoolhouse and didn't even bother to post guards.

The next day, December 23, they went out on routine patrol and ran into sixty tanks of the 2nd Panzer Division. The flustered squadron commander radioed, "What the hell are these tanks doing here? I thought we were a hundred miles from the nearest Kraut." It was only then that he and his men learned the Battle of the Bulge had been under way for eight days.

Snafu.

As for Lisa, Freddie, and me, we hadn't reached that stage yet. That is, not until we met Miller and Marcus.

I never knew their first names—they called one another Miller and Marcus. Both were buck sergeants. Both were about six feet tall, both were muscular, both were dark and intense looking with surburban New York accents. In fact, Miller and Marcus were almost interchangeable.

We literally ran into them.

The children and I had left the cabin in the *Forêt de Freyr* at about 6 P.M. on the evening of December 23, and without too much trouble I had found the new road cut through the woods by Ray's band of AWOL black marketeers. It wasn't really a road, just a short connection between the trail leading to the cabin and another trail heading west, but at least the brush had been pushed aside and the larger trees circumvented.

138

When I reached the westbound trail, I doused my head-lights and felt my way by the faint illumination of the stars and a tiny sliver of a moon. The one thing I didn't want to do was barge out onto the St. Hubert highway, which, I knew, was well within Kraut-held territory.

At about seven o'clock I heard sporadic traffic on a paved road just ahead. I cut the engine and coasted downhill at a crawl along the trail. It had turned much colder. The snow had packed down hard in the ruts, leaving a comparatively smooth surface.

Suddenly I felt the front of the jeep hit something silently and bounce back. At first I thought it was a tree, but then I recalled that trees weren't that resilient.

My heart did a little bounce.

There was just enough dim light for me to realize that I had hit the rear-mounted spare tire of another jeep, parked half on the trail and half in the underbrush.

From the darkness came a fearsome sputtering: "What the fuck was that?"

A second voice said, "I don't know, I was working on the radiator and something just knocked me on my ass."

"Hey, Mac," I yelled. "I'm an American. Here. Just behind you."

Two flashlights switched on and two dour faces looked in on me and the children. The bumpees weren't taking any chances. They both held cocked .45's. They held them until I had explained who I was and what we were doing there.

And that's how we met Miller and Marcus.

What they were doing there was almost as odd a story as mine. They were noncoms in a SHAEF headquarters detach-ment, whose most recent mission was to capture Radio Lux-embourg and then to provide security for the Psychological Warfare Company sent in to use the transmitter, one of the world's most powerful, for propaganda broadcasts against the Germans. The Krauts had done the same with Radio Luxembourg, in reverse, since 1940.

On December 15, Miller and Marcus had been reassigned to Paris. They had taken off in their jeep on December 16 and immediately been caught up in the chaos caused by the German breakthrough in the Schnee Eifel. They had found themselves isolated north of the shattered American 106th Division, stopped to do some fighting at St. Vith when they were ordered into action by a U.S. one-star General at a crossroads, got cut off again by the Krauts south of Bastogne, and finally ended up in the *Forêt de Freyr* that evening.

Now, their jeep was useless. The radiator had frozen and burst. The antifreeze long since had evaporated, and they had replaced it with water.

Miller and Marcus seemed to take me at face value, but I was a lot cagier with them. My previous encounters had taught me a few techniques. I mentioned that I had done a story on the Psychological Warfare Company at Radio Luxembourg—which I had—and I asked, as innocently as I could, "Do you fellows speak German?"

Miller grumbled, "Had to. Those guys in the Psych Company were so fresh out of Deutschland that most of them couldn't hardly speak English yet."

That was true. The Psychological Warfare outfit was made up of soldiers who were recent German refugees, mostly Jewish. They were selected not because of their proficiency with English, which many of them had not completely mastered, but for their ability to speak flawless and unaccented German in their propaganda broadcasts.

I persisted, however. "The captain of that outfit—what was his name again, Horner?"

"No," Marcus said drily. "Habe."

"A little short fellow?"

"No, tall."

"A poet?"

"No, he was a novelist."

"But there was a shortish, husky fellow, a corporal—"

"Yeah," Marcus said, "Peter Wyden."

It all checked. I was thinking up some more tricky questions when Miller said, "Why don't we cut out this bullshit, Mac, and decide what we're going to do. Our jeep is shot. Can we ride with you and these kids in yours?"

I was abashed that my interrogation methods had been seen through as bullshit, but glad they had worked. "Sure."

"All right, then," said Marcus, taking charge. He flashed his light into the back of my jeep. "The first thing we've got to do is get rid of a lot of this shit back here. Right, Miller?"

"Right," said Miller.

"Why?" I asked. "It took me a lot of time to collect that shit."

"Because," Marcus said patiently, "we have to make room for two more asses. Besides, you got enough food for a month and the way we figure it, we should be inside our own lines in about twenty-four hours."

"O.K.," I said grudgingly. And I watched as my Dutch cookies, my Danish chocolate, even my Throne were tossed out into the snow.

Miller and Marcus then walked over to their own jeep and returned with two barracks bags which they squeezed into the cleared areas in the back. Miller had a heavy piece of equipment slung over his shoulder.

"What's that?" I asked.

"A field radio."

"Can you hear the Krauts on that as well as our guys?"

"Goddam right," he said. "That's how we got this far. We go where they ain't."

I remembered that these were the same words used by Ray's men about their field radio, and I was euphoric. All of that depressing day before in the cabin I had worried about the way I kept running into misanthropes like myself who didn't know their ass from a rifle barrel. Why couldn't I find some genuine experienced soldiers for a change who could help me get out of this mess? The black marketeers had come closest. They were efficient and field-intuitive; but they weren't soldiers, they were stockade bait. I had said to myself, "If I only could run into guys who were just as smart—but straight."

And here they were.

"How do you think we should ride?" I asked Marcus.

"You drive," he said. "The kids stay in the front. We'll ride in the back and tell you where to go. One of us will spell you at the wheel once in a while."

"Which way do we head?"

"Go to the St. Hubert road. We'll stop there and scout it for traffic. Once we get across, we'll have to find trails in the woods again until we reach the Nassogne road. Then we go west until we run into the 335th Infantry."

It was the first time in three years that I appreciated military forcefulness. Before I started the jeep, I nudged the children happily.

Lisa rubbed her face against my sleeve, but otherwise the kids didn't respond very much. From their total silence the preceding several minutes, I sensed that they weren't overly fond of Miller and Marcus. Which got me slightly pissed off.

They had fawned over every ass-hole we had met along the way. But Miller and Marcus, two real soldiers, they didn't like.

19

Miller and Marcus were good, very good. After we had found no traffic on the St. Hubert highway and crossed it, we proceeded on a rigid military schedule through the western finger of the *Forêt de Freyr* pointing toward Rochefort. We moved ahead for twenty-five minutes and then stopped and rested for five.

The Great Forest was even thicker and wilder here than on the other side of the St. Hubert highway; the trails even more difficult to find. Miller and Marcus took turns walking ahead and signaling to me with quick blinks on their flashlights. I noted that each was armed with a carbine as well as his .45.

At one point, I got three quick blinks from Marcus—the prearranged signal for danger. I turned off the ignition, and we froze. For a few agonizing moments I heard nothing, and then the crunch of about a dozen footsteps in the snow—faintly, off in the distance. The footsteps stopped. Then they continued again, moving away from us.

I got the one-blink signal from Marcus to move forward again. About a hundred feet further on, he materialized along-side the jeep. "What was it?" I whispered.

"A *maquis* patrol," he whispered back. "They're letting us through."

I wanted to ask him how far it was to the edge of the Great Forest, but he had disappeared again.

During the five-minute breaks, he and Miller were almost totally noncommunicative. For instance, I brought up the subject of the *maquis* patrol and asked him if he spoke French as well as German.

"Uh-huh," he said.

"Where did you learn it?"

"Cornell."

And that was typical of our conversations.

The children slept most of the time, but during the five-minute breaks they were restive. Freddie's raw rash obviously pained him chronically now, and he squirmed around under the sleeping bag, trying to find a comfortable position. Lisa had to go to the bathroom as frequently as usual. She sobbed, the first time, when I told her she didn't have the Throne to use any more. I tried to explain to her why we had had to jettison it. Miller and Marcus listened with amusement. Then Miller said something to Lisa in quick, expert German that I couldn't even follow.

Lisa stared at him in amazement and dutifully went off to squat down in the woods. When she came back, she cuddled next to me closer than ever.

From time to time, during the breaks, Miller pulled out the long antenna of his radio pack, put on a pair of earphones, and turned the dials of the radio. I could hear whispered snatches of conversation between him and Marcus:

"I can't pick up the 335th. Where the fuck are they?"

"I think this is Panzer Lehr. What's their code name again?"

"It sounds like the 116th Panzer is trying to break through to the 2nd Panzer at Celles, but I think they've run into Combat Command A of the Second Armored."

We reached the edge of the *Forêt de Freyr* at about ten o'clock. It had taken us three hours to go no more than six miles. It was quite a heady feeling, though, like getting out of prison. At that moment I didn't know if maybe the fir prison wasn't better, but the claustrophobia dropped away as I looked at the open fields, fairly visible now under the sliver of moon which had risen higher in the sky.

In fact, it all was beautiful. The fields seemed level and peaceful under their glistening white mantle. It hadn't snowed as heavily here, and there were bare patches of dark earth amid the white. Off to the left, I could see the ruin of a stone farmhouse. That spoiled the tableau. From listening to Miller and Marcus, I gathered that it was a recently created ruin.

Marcus pointed to the western horizon. It was glowing red. "Shit," he said.

"What is it?" I asked.

"Rochefort."

He then ignored me and consulted with Miller.

"Do you think it was Panzer Lehr?" I heard him say.

"Yeah, they must have shelled it," he said. "They need those river crossings over the Lisse and the Lomme."

"I thought the 335th was holding Rochefort."

"They were. I think Panzer Lehr must be in the town by now."

"What about the 3rd Battalion of the 335th? Didn't they set up a line this side of Rochefort?"

Miller flashed his light briefly on a map he was holding. "Yeah," he said. "About two-seven-five degrees from here. Slightly north of west."

"O.K.," said Marcus, "let's head that way."

I had seen what appeared to be a road just beyond the first row of fields. It looked to me as if it ran east and west. "How do we go?" I asked. "On the road?"

"No," Marcus said, "it may be mined. We cut across the fields."

I nodded and started the engine. Marcus said, "Wait. Miller better drive now."

"Why?" I said.

"Because the gate paths between the fields may be mined, too. I'll walk ahead and check them. You get in the back with

145

the kids. Put all the duffle bags on the floor and sit on top of them. Then, if we hit something, the duffle bags will absorb a lot of the impact and you won't get hurt so bad."

That was the most he had said at one time in three hours —but it was enough. I got in the back of the jeep and perched on the duffle bags. I held the children in my lap. At least, then, my ass would take the mine fragments and not their's. I was more terrified than I had been since Schloss Hemingstein, but I was beginning to get used to it. A dull feeling of nausea was becoming a constant state with me.

We began to move across the fields. At each gate crossing, Marcus would kneel down, scratch gingerly at the dirt and snow, and wave us through.

We had proceeded this way for about twenty minutes—it seemed like hours—when we came to a darkened village. We skirted the village and kept going. About three fields beyond, Marcus waved us to a stop with his flashlight. He played his light on a little patch of woods, and against the dark background I could see a twisted mass of burned out military vehicles. They all had the white star of the U.S. Army on them. My nose picked up the all too familiar stench of dead bodies.

Marcus waved us on. The further we went, the more unbearable became the stench. I tried to cover the children's noses with my scarf—a chunk of nylon parachute—and I told them to breathe through their mouths. But they began to whimper, and I couldn't get them to stop.

Finally we came to a field in which there seemed to be more bare earth patches in the snow than usual. We didn't need the flashlight now to tell us what the patches were. There was enough light from burning Rochefort, only a couple of miles away.

The patches were bodies.

Along a tree line bordering the field was a row of fox holes. There were more bodies, some of them half in and half out of the holes.

146

Marcus turned to Miller and said, "Well, that'll give you some idea of what happened to the 335th."

"Yeah," said Miller. "No wonder I couldn't pick 'em up on the radio."

"What do we do *now?*" I said.

"It beats the shit outta me, Mac, but we'll figure something out," said Marcus. "The first thing is we got to get away from this fuckin' smell."

Three fields further on the ultimate body odor had dissipated to the point where at least we could breathe normally again. Miller stopped the jeep in the shadows beside a culvert, and he and Marcus consulted. Miller listened to his radio for a while; Marcus checked his maps.

I heard Miller say, "The Bridge at Han is out, so we can't cross the river there."

Marcus said, "Any other river crossings?"

"Not on this side of Rochefort."

"Any place we can ford the river?"

"No, it's too deep."

I interjected, "Why can't we just hole up somewhere out here in the country, like I've been doing all along?"

"Impossible," said Marcus. "Panzer Lehr is busy now mopping up north of Rochefort. They've got to secure another bridge to the north that's more important to them than the little one in the town. Tomorrow, this area will be swarming with Krauts."

"Then what are *we* going to do?" I asked.

"We're going to go right through Rochefort," he said, "and cross that little old bridge."

As the jeep crawled across the fields to the outskirts of Rochefort, I tried to distract my mind from fear by thinking of everything I could remember about the town. It was actually a small city, totally unlike the ancient agriculture-based towns further east. Whenever I had passed through Rochefort,

147

it had reminded me of commuter bedroom communities like Larchmont, outside of New York City, and Forest Park, near Chicago. It had a lot of châteaux and modern brick homes, and, as I later learned, it indeed was a commuter bedroom community. It was within thirty miles of the industrial cities of Namur and Huy, in the Meuse River Valley, and a lot of the executives and supervisory personnel of the paper mills, brass and iron works, and tanneries drove to work there from Rochefort every day. There even was a respectable businessmen's bar in the Hotel Central in Rochefort, where the commuters stopped off for a quick belt before going home at night.

The town was new, I guessed, because it had been in the way of the massive German bombardment of Namur in 1914. It made a startling contrast with its sister city of Marche-en-Famenne, just eight miles away. In Marche-en-Famenne, when you ask about their famous church, listed in the guidebooks, they ask politely, "The new church or the old church?" The old church, at Waha, was built A.D. 1000. The new church is a johnny-come-lately, dating only from the 1500's.

Once we reached the outlying houses of Rochefort, all thoughts of churches and commuters left my mind. This southern edge of town seemed to be the hardest hit by the German shelling. In the dancing light of flames from the burning buildings, I could see a lot of civilians scurrying around. There was also a lot of muted yelling. I heard the claxons of the local firemen, the *pompiers,* but with the water supply probably shut down, I didn't figure they could do much good—except maybe to pull the dead and injured out of the shelled buildings.

Marcus, who was driving, seemed to know where he was going. He turned into a street that was untouched by the shelling and then into a side road. He found a brick house with a nice piece of land around it and went up a driveway to the rear of the house, where there was an old stone barn that had been converted into a garage. He drove right into the garage alongside a Renault that hadn't been used in a long time. It was up on blocks.

Marcus got out of the jeep. "I know this lady," he said, and strode off to the house.

We waited for him in the jeep for about twenty minutes. The children were terrified by the distant shouting and the claxons. I rested their heads on my lap and tried to soothe them by rubbing the backs of their necks. I wanted to ask Miller how Marcus knew the lady in the house, but Miller had got out of the jeep and was prowling around outside the garage.

Marcus came back, adjusting the fly on his pants as he walked. I thought, My God, did he get laid at a time like this? But then I gave him the benefit of the doubt and figured that he had just taken a leak. I didn't get a chance to ask him one way or the other, because he immediately had a quick conversation with Miller.

"She doesn't know much," said Marcus. "She's been afraid to leave the house since the shelling. All she could tell me was that what was left of the 335th pulled out of town when Panzer Lehr came through. She doesn't have any idea of what's going on in Rochefort right now, except that most of the fighting seems to be a little further north, along the river."

Miller and Marcus whipered together for a minute or so and I couldn't hear them.

Marcus came over to me. He looked thoughtful. "You speak good French, don't you?"

I nodded.

"Well, there's something you've got to do."

"What's that?"

"Walk up to that street up ahead where the big fire is and mingle with the crowd. Try to find out if there are any Krauts on the main drag past the Hotel Central which leads to the bridge."

"But why me?"

"We've got other things to do here, like checking the radio. Besides, you could pass as a civilian Belgian correspondent from Brussels, just accredited since the liberation."

"But my accent?"

"Say you were educated in Quebec. To them, anyone who speaks funny French is a French Canadian."

I hesitated. "Haul ass," said Marcus. "It's our only chance." I started to get out of the jeep. Lisa grabbed me, crying, and she said, as she had outside the whorehouse several days before, "Papa, *nicht gehen.*" Marcus said something to her in his quick German, and she relaxed her hold on me and let go. But I noticed that both she and Freddie stared at Marcus again in wonder.

I walked down the dark streets, staying in the shadows, trying to make myself as unobtrusive as possible. Some of my flagging courage returned when people rushed past in twos and threes, paying no attention to me whatsoever.

The light from the flames got brighter and finally I turned a corner into the area that had been hard hit by the shelling. The scene sickened me, though it was exactly the same as those I had seen in London, Antwerp, a dozen other towns. There was fire and rubble and bodies and parts of bodies; smoke and the choking dust of collapsed buildings. There was screaming and yelling and scurrying. There was the inevitable spectacle of a hysterical woman clawing at the rubble above a pair of child's legs protruding from it. It always sickened me.

I wandered around the edge of the screaming crowd. The *pompiers* were using some sort of chemical from a tank truck to try and extinguish the flames in what may have been a school or a church. Their efforts weren't accomplishing very much. Neither were those of a chain of men and women who had formed a bucket bridgade. The rest of the people in the street were digging in the rubble. I was totally ignored.

I saw an old man sitting on what had been the stone fence

in front of one of the larger buildings. He was rocking sadly back and forth, but he seemed considerably less hysterical than the others. He wore the lapel button of a World War I Belgian Army veteran.

I sat down beside him.

He glanced at my shoulder patch. *"Américain?"*

"Non, Belge," I said, and added hastily that my education had been in Quebec.

He nodded, as if this were the most natural thing in the world. "Yes," he said in French, "before the war, a friend of mine in Brussels dispatched his son to study at the University of McGill. The son, unfortunately, was killed in the great raid on Dieppe with Mountbatten."

We continued the conversation, and he completely accepted my accented French. "The Americans," I said, "they are all gone from Rochefort?"

"Yes, they fought bravely against the great odds of the Boche tanks, but in the end, the survivors withdrew to the west. A friend of mine who is in the *maquis* informs me that they crossed the Lisse beyond Han and successfully arrived at Givet, on the Meuse, which the British hold with great firmness."

I had a wild flash of hope that we might follow the same escape route to Givet. The old man quickly dashed it. "The Americans," he said, "successfully blew up the Lisse bridge behind them, so that the Boche tanks could not follow."

"Are there many Boches in Rochefort tonight?"

"Not many. Most are engaged in fighting for the big bridge to the north."

"How many in Rochefort?"

"An occasional patrol. A few at the small bridge. Tomorrow I am sure they will return in force."

That's all I could get out of the old man. His attention wandered as he resumed his rocking and watched the attempts to put out the fires. I gave him some Wings cigarettes I car-

151

ried in the side pocket of my trench coat, and headed back to where the jeep was waiting.

At least I hoped it was waiting. I had a nervous fear that sending me for information had been a ruse to enable Miller and Marcus to abscond with my precious vehicle. Then a really terrifying thought hit me: if they did take off with the jeep, what would they do with the children?

I began to run.

I reached the garage totally out of breath and flung myself inside.

"What the fuck's the matter with you?" said Marcus. He and Miller and the children were all sitting there, placidly eating K-ration chocolate.

20

When my respiration had returned to normal, I told Miller and Marcus what I had learned from the old man.

"That's good," Marcus said. "I figure now we've got a better than even chance of getting through the town."

"How so?" I asked. "What about the patrols and the detachment at the bridge?"

"Leave that to us."

He walked over to the back of the jeep and pulled out his duffle bag and Miller's. Rummaging in the duffle bags, he came up with what seemed to be two flowing white capes with hoods attached. "What in hell are those?" I asked him.

"Those," he said, "are German snow-camouflage suits. The Krauts learned about them from the Russkies and they used them for the first time in the snow here in the West in this offensive."

"Where did you get them?"

Miller was holding them up, examining some blood stains and bullet holes with his flashlight. "St. Vith."

"From dead Krauts?"

"You can bet your ass we didn't take 'em off live ones." Miller turned to Marcus. "I told you these might come in handy some day," he said.

They slipped the white camouflage suits on over their uniforms, helmets and all. I had a pretty good idea what they had in mind but I insisted that they spell it out for me.

Miller explained patiently: "Look, Mac, as far as we know there's only one bridge for us to get across this fuckin' river. The bridge happens to be in this town. In order to get to the bridge and across it, we have to go through the town. Right now, the town is kind of a no-man's-land, with only a few patrols. But even so, do you you want us to go through the town looking like Krauts, or do you want us to go through the town looking like Americans?"

"But the jeep," I protested. "It's an American vehicle with a white star on it."

Marcus broke in. "Forget that," he said. "While you were gone we picked up some good information on the radio. Half the Kraut army is using American vehicles. All their gasoline is going to their tanks. With their cars and trucks, when they run out of gas or break down, the Krauts just pick up a U.S. jeep or a four-by-four and keep going. Our guys are leaving vehicles all over the place. When the 335th pulled out, they must have abandoned about a hundred here in Rochefort alone."

I was scared, but I wanted my fear to sound like indignation. For some reason, I seized on the ridiculous idea that I was a Staff Sergeant and they were only three-stripers.

"Listen to me, you guys," I said. "I outrank both of you and this is a half-assed idea. I don't mind risking my life with this crazy gamble, but what about the kids? (I suddenly realized through my personal fear that I really meant that.) I went on, "Couldn't we just stay here and let the Belgians hide us?"

Marcus shrugged. "Suit yourself," he said. "But just remember that tomorrow the Panzer Lehr Division comes back, and they set up the division headquarters in Rochefort, and with division headquarters comes the Gestapo."

154

With that one sentence, all the force of my argument collapsed.

"All right. How do we work this thing with the camouflage suits and the jeep?"

"Miller and I are in the suits, and we ride up front," said Marcus. "You and the kids lay low in the back—under the barracks bags, if possible. All you have to do is keep the kids quiet."

I still had a tiny speck of indignation left. "You're the one who speaks German so well," I said. "You tell them."

He spoke to the children, who listened gravely and looked up at me for confirmation. I nodded, and they walked dutifully over to the back of the jeep for me to help them in.

It was impossible for us to get under the barracks bags, but we coiled ourselves around and made as low a profile as possible. Miller spread my sleeping bag over us. The children were surprisingly stoic and quiet.

I heard the jeep's engine start and felt it back out of the garage and the driveway into the road. Then we were moving forward at a pretty good pace.

We passed an area of screaming and yelling and claxons. I guessed it was the spot where I had done my reconnoitering. Then there was quiet, soon followed by more screaming and yelling. We made a left turn and did some intricate twists and turns. I figured we were working our way through piles of rubble. The smoke and the dust and the odor of burning human flesh penetrated the sleeping bag that covered us. The children coughed. I had to nudge them to be still.

We moved along at a pretty good pace for a few minutes and swung into a wide right turn. This would be the corner where the Hotel Central stood, with its commuters' café. So far, nobody had stopped us. I was beginning to breathe a little more easily—even with the smoke and the dust and the children's breath in my face as they huddled in the crook of my body.

Then came those dreaded German words, *"Halt machen!"* The jeep stopped. We must be at the bridge. The children were trembling, and, I realized, so was I. I tasted sour C-ration in my throat.

The German voices asked questions and I caught the glint of a flashlight around the edge of the spread-out sleeping bag. I heard Miller and Marcus answering in their fast German.

Suddenly there was a great roar of laughter. Maybe six people seemed to be laughing, including Miller and Marcus.

The next thing I knew, I felt the jeep's transmission engage. For a moment, I was so tense and confused that I didn't know whether we were going backward or forward.

Another confused moment later, I realized we were moving ahead. We were crossing the bridge.

At the other end there were a few more German voices, this time perfunctory; we slowed down for them but did not stop. We rolled along smoothly for a while. By now my legs and back were so cramped that I thought I'd lose my mind if I couldn't straighten up soon. Then both legs fell asleep. I must have begun to squirm, because I felt Miller's hand on me in a silent warning to stay where I was, and stay still.

I tried to think of all sorts of pleasant things to keep my mind off the maddening knots in my back and pins and needles in my legs. I ended up marveling about the bravery of the children, who hadn't stirred since we passed the roadblock at the bridge.

The jeep began to slow down, bounced over some uneven ground, and came to a dead stop. I thought we had come to another German roadblock, but then Marcus' voice said, "O.K., you can come out now."

The children and I crawled out of our nest in the back of the jeep. My legs were so weak I couldn't stand up, and I had to hold onto the side of the vehicle for a few minutes before any feeling returned to them.

I looked around. Miller and Marcus were smoking and talking quietly. We were in a small patch of woods, beyond which, even in the faint moonlight, I could see rolling open farmland. Perfect tank country, I thought. I looked at my watch: 2:25 A.M. We had left our refuge in the *Forêt de Freyr* only eight-and-a-half hours before.

The children had to go to the bathroom, and so did I, once I had regained the use of my legs. My nervous colon finally erupted, and I suffered through a long bout of diarrhea. When I got back to the jeep, Miller and Marcus were staring at me with amusement. The children were eating K-ration chocolate again.

Miller and Marcus offered me a cigarette—a real Gauloise —and after I'd smoked it, I settled down somewhat.

"Say, what was it back at the bridge that was so funny?" I asked them.

"I told the guards we were on a special mission across the river," Marcus said. "For old Iron-ass Bayerlein—to bring him back a particularly luscious piece of tail he had enjoyed when he was in Rochefort before, during the Occupation."

"And who the fuck is Iron-ass Bayerlein?"

"Generalleutnant Fritz Bayerlein. Commanding General of Hitler's own Panzer Lehr Division."

We rested for a while in the little patch of woods. I noticed that the tall menacing firs were gone. These trees were birch, oak, and ash, and their dead fallen leaves crackled underfoot beneath the thin layer of snow. The reappearance of the deciduous trees was somewhat reassuring. They reminded me of New England, where I had taken long automobile trips on sunlit winter weekends. Here, under the Belgian moon sliver, I could even see a New England-like church steeple on the horizon.

A Marcus pun stirred me out of my reverie. "Let's get going," he said. "We're not out of the woods *yet*."

21

I went over to where the children were standing. They were crunching the dead leaves with their feet and seemed to be enjoying the sound. They were, in fact, hopping up and down on the leaves like kids in a New England playground. It was hard to believe they had just run a German roadblock hidden under a Fortnum and Mason sleeping bag.

I checked Lisa's nylon stockings. The skin beneath the sheer fabric was pink, not blue, so my improvisation must be doing its job fairly well. Lisa did a pirouette, and I said, *"Nein,* I don't have to *examiner* your new *culottes."*

I then checked Freddie's rash. It looked horrible. "Do you guys happen to have any antiseptic ointment?" I asked Miller.

"Sure," he said, "Why didn't you ask us before?" He reached into a first-aid kit and threw me a tube of zinc oxide. Freddie winced at the first sting as I applied the white paste, but then it seemed to soothe him. He went back to stamping on the leaves with Lisa.

Miller and Marcus were stuffing their German snow-camouflage suits back into their barracks bags, so I walked over to the jeep. Of all the treasures that once had been in the *Lootwagen,* only a single case of rations remained. I felt a twinge of regret, and then somehow I didn't mind. The portable cache of luxuries was not that important anymore. I had learned how easily I could get by on much less when the crucial thing was to remain alive—by the most primitive means, if necessary. I even had come to appreciate C-and-K-ration. It still tasted horrible, but it filled the stomach and kept you going.

Miller and Marcus came over and tossed their barracks bags into the jeep, then climbed in after them.

"You can drive now," said Marcus. "Keep the kids up front with you."

"What about the mines?"

"There won't be any here."

"How so?"

"The Second Panzer came through so fast they didn't have time. They pulled in their tail after them, and now they're bunched up in two pockets at Celles and Foy Notre-Dame, about twelve miles from here."

"What about other Kraut outfits?"

"They're stopped back at the river north of Rochefort. So far, neither Panzer Lehr or the Ninth Panzer have been able to break through to join up with the Second Panzer. They ran into our Seventh Corps."

"Can I stick to the roads?"

"Sure, for now. When we get closer to where we're going, one of us will take over at the wheel. Now that we've gone through all this, we don't want to get shot up by our own people."

"Where are we going?"

"Toward Ciney. The American Second Armored's there."

"How do you know all this? From the radio?"

He nodded. I asked him something that had been preying on my mind for a long time. "Say, can you talk on that thing as well as listen?"

"I wish we could," he said. "We might've been out of this a long time ago. What we have is a monitoring set. It's designed just to listen, not to transmit."

I wasn't quite sure, but since Miller was in an unusually

loquacious mood, I pressed the point. "You mean it isn't a walkie-talkie?"

"No, we started out with a walkie-talkie too, but it got shot up at St. Vith. An 88 fragment sliced it—just over Marcus' right ear."

He made a gesture of impatience, indicating that I should shut up and drive. Which I proceeded to do.

My notes indicate that we drove toward Buissonville, took a crossroads left to Houyet, passed through the villages of Chevetogne and Mont Gauthier, and finally reached Ver-Custinne. From what I could see of the countryside, it had changed radically. We did go through what a sign told us was a National Forest, but the rest of it was much more tailored than anything I had seen in days. The patches of woods were fewer, the rolling farmland was much richer looking, the hills more rounded and planted with grass instead of trees. Ver-Custinne actually was on a flat plain, not unlike those in France. There were scarcely any stone houses any more. Most were built out of twentieth-century brick.

But then I couldn't see anything. The moon had set and an early morning haze blanked out the stars. Marcus made me drive with just the blue black-out headlights. So I was back to my old routine of groping my way along—for at least an hour.

The children dropped off to sleep. As time went by, Miller and Marcus grew increasingly nervous. Marcus kept looking at his watch, which had a luminescent dial. At about 5 A.M., when a little pink light began to speckle the eastern sky, I heard him say, "Shit!"

"What's the matter?"

"Daylight, that's what's the matter. We can't go running around on this open plain when the sun comes up. Some trigger-happy GI ass-hole will cut us down with a bazooka, or"—he looked up at the sky, which already was beginning to buzz with the sound of distant aircraft—"one of those jerks might decide to have himself a turkey shoot with a single jeep that's not supposed to be here."

He scanned the horizon, beginning to emerge in the growing light, and pointed to a tree line between two fields, about a quarter of a mile away. "Over there," he ordered. I turned the jeep to the right and across an open pasture.

When we got to the tree line it turned out to be a hedgerow, like those which had restricted the fighting in Normandy, an ancient earthen wall, four feet high or so, with trees planted along its top. These trees seemed to be locusts.

"Pretty piss-poor shelter," Marcus grumbled, "but at least they're not those skinny poplars. They won't be able to see us from the air, anyway."

I found a cattle path cut in the hedgerow and pulled through it to the other side—away from the road. I snuggled the jeep as close as I could against the hedgerow. It wasn't too good. The jeep was hidden from the road, but if we stood up, we weren't. I wished the hedgerow were one of the six-foot variety.

So, presumably, did Marcus. "Christ," he said, "and we might have to stay here until nightfall." He thought for a minute, and then said unexpectedly, "Say what day is it, anyway?" I had been keeping a calendar in my notebook.

It was the morning of Sunday, December 24. Christmas Eve.

Marcus didn't explain why he wanted to know. "All right, the three of us will have to pull guard," he said. "Two hours on and one hour off." He looked at me, probably sensing that I was a novice at such matters. "Keep your head just over the top of the hedgerow. No helmet, and stay behind one of the trees. If you see any GI's on the road, stand up and yell as loud as you can and wave your fuckin' arms. If you see any Belgians, try to get them to get the word to the nearest unit that we're out here."

Just as he finished I heard another voice, so closely following Marcus' that I thought it was an echo.

The voice was deep and resonant and it was saying, in English, "Well, lookee here."

It belonged to an enormous GI with corporal's stripes, who was standing on the hedgerow behind Marcus' head. The M-1 rifle he was carrying seemed no bigger than a riding crop as he cradled it in his giant arms. He was staring with utter incredulity at Lisa and her baggy nylons.

Behind him, down the hedgerow, a patrol of seven more GI's kept popping up—like tenpins returning to position in a bowling alley. They, too, were staring in bewilderment—first at the children, then at us.

They all wore the colorful triangular shoulder patch of the U.S. Second Armored Division, also known as "Hell on Wheels." They were scruffy and dirty, and I had never been so glad to see anybody in my life.

But, looking down at the kids I'd soon have to give up, I also knew that my own ordeal was far from over.

22

We were passed through the chain of command—from platoon to company to battalion. At both the company and battalion command posts, I was interrogated by S-2 Intelligence officers, each of whom expressed a certain amount of disbelief at my story, but on seeing my *Yank* credentials they let me proceed to the rear. By now I was so tired and so relieved that I didn't care what they thought. All I remember is that we finally ended up in the crowded basement of a church, where some kindly Belgian women took over the care of the children. I fell asleep on the floor and slept until late that afternoon. I don't know what Miller and Marcus were doing.

When I awakened, however, they were there.

"What's going on?" I asked Marcus.

"We're in the town of Achene," he said, "but we can't get out of here until tomorrow. The roads are clogged. A whole combat command of the Second Armored is coming down from Ciney. They're going to attack the Kraut Second Panzer in that pocket I told you about at Celles. That's the high point of the German offensive, but they're cut off there and out of gas. It ought to be quite a shooting gallery."

I shrugged and looked around for the children, who were asleep on the floor beside me. Someone had spread a green satin quilt under them and covered them with a rose-colored blanket.

With their blue knitted caps peeking out between the quilt and the blanket, they were a colorful pair.

Miller and Marcus wandered off again and I looked around the basement room. It was milling with people now, and I guessed that the MP's had herded the entire civilian population of the village down there. The structure had heavy masonry walls and sturdy oak beams and probably was the safest place in town.

The civilians were remarkably well organized and considerably more sophisticated than the mainly-peasant population further east. I heard people referred to as *Monsieur le docteur* and *Monsieur le professeur*. Highly efficient-looking ladies had organized a nursery in one corner of the room and were keeping the older children occupied with books and drawing pads. Others were operating a chow line from a long table set up in the middle of the room. I wandered over to the chow line and had an excellent paté sandwich and coffee.

While I was eating the sandwich, one of the nursery ladies came over to talk to me. She was middle-aged, and with her pouter-pigeon figure encased in a dark blue dress she looked like a schoolteacher. She spoke cultured Brussels French.

"Your children, monsieur," she said, "are both brave and spirited."

I felt a glow of pride, but I sensed that some sort of confrontation had taken place between Freddie and Lisa and the woman. "Thank you," I said. "What is it that has caused you to reach this evaluation of the children?"

She knew exactly what I was driving at. She smiled and said, "Yes, monsieur, there was a small contretemps, but nothing serious, I assure you." I had a pretty good idea of what was coming.

"The little girl's stockings?"

The woman smiled again. "Yes, monsieur, how did you know?"

"Instinct," I said. "But tell me what happened."

166

"I attempted to remove the stockings and replace them with a pair of my niece's, who is about the same age. Now, mind you, the nylon stockings are beautiful and I wish I had a pair of my own, but as you know, they do not fit the little girl." She was very polite. She didn't ask me where and how I had obtained the nylons for Lisa.

"Anyway," the woman went on, "when I attempted to remove the nylon stockings and fit the little girl with the good black woolen ones, she would not permit me. At first I was angry, but then I remembered what the Sergeant, Monsieur Miller, had told me." She shuddered. "God help us," she said. "A Jewish child from Germany."

She continued, after a pause. "I thought to myself, *pauvre petite,* these ridiculously large nylon stockings must be the first new clothing, the first real possession she ever has had."

I hadn't thought of it that way and it broke me up, but I knew it wasn't the whole story of why Lisa wanted to cling so desperately to the nylons. "You are very wise, madame," I said, "but what solution did you arrive at in the end? I'm sure you did find a solution."

"A compromise," she said. "We decided that the little girl would retain her nylon stockings but would wear them inside the good black woolen ones. And so it was arranged. The nylon stockings, though large, are quite flimsy and fit with rectitude within the woolen stockings. There is a bulge here and there, but mostly beneath her skirt, and therefore quite unnoticeable. The child was very happy with our little arrangement," she added triumphantly.

"And the little boy? Were there difficulties with him as well?"

"He was not so obstinate, but yes, there was the matter of his underclothing. He was wearing *caleçons* of Army cloth that seem to have been sewn together by a drunken cobbler."

"Yes, I know," I said.

"*Monsieur le docteur* had to remove the drawers in order to treat the little boy's rash. He bathed and cleaned the area and insisted that I find other drawers to replace those upon the little boy. The little boy would accede only if I returned to him his old drawers, which were soiled with stains of blood and pus. So I laundered the drawers and the little boy now has them, still wet, in the pocket of his overcoat. The nylons I can understand, but a disgusting tatter such as the drawers I cannot."

"Madame," I said gently, "certainly by now we both know that the quirks of children's minds sometimes cannot be explained. They have their own secrets."

"You are correct," she said. "Sometimes I forget that, although I teach them every day in the school."

She was a good woman.

"Monsieur," she said, "the doctor told me to tell you that the boy needs further medical attention when you arrive at the refugee center in Dinant. That is where you are taking the children, I presume?"

"If that is the nearest refugee center, that is where I will take them. I thank you for the information. And you are very kind."

The woman hesitated for a moment and said, "Monsieur, one other matter, if I may be so bold as to suggest. We have here in the village a childless couple, teachers like myself. Perhaps, since the children are orphans, you could permit them to stay here with this couple, who are good citizens and who always have grieved because they do not have a son and daughter of their own. I know the children are Jews, but if they were raised as Christians, it is the same God, no?"

I was deeply touched by the suggestion and I thought about it for several minutes. Finally I said, "You are extremely kind, madame, but I fear I cannot do what you suggest. It is not a matter of the religion. It is a matter of the possibility that somewhere in the world these children may have an uncle or an aunt, perhaps an older brother or sister, who are grieving. It is my responsibility to deliver the children to the proper authorities who have the machinery to locate any relatives, so they can be raised with their own people. These children have suffered enough and have known only strangers."

The woman nodded. "You are right, monsieur," she said, "and you, too, are extremely kind."

It being Christmas Eve, there was an impromptu mass in the basement of the church at midnight. After that, there was very little sleep for anyone as the tanks and the artillery of the Second Armored began to roar and clank along the cobbled street overhead.

They were moving into the line for the crucial Battle of Celles, which was to take place in the open plain just a couple of miles down the road.

I saw nothing of this battle. I stayed in the basement of the church with the children and the panicky civilians.

Some GI's, however, climbed to the steeples of this church and others for a bird's-eye view of at least the initial stages of the great clash of armor. One of the GI's, T-5 Melvin Grayson of the Fourth Cavalry, told me about it many years later, when he was an executive for *Look* Magazine:

"We had held the town overnight for the Second Armored, and early in the morning of Christmas Day they came through to relieve us. It was Combat Command B of the division, commanded by a one-star general, Isaac White, I believe. I never saw so many American tanks in one place at one time. There probably were only about fifty of them, with half-tracks and supporting artillery, but at the time it seemed as if there were hundreds. It was the one-star general who suggested that we go up into the church steeple to watch—almost like he was about to stage a performance and wanted an appreciative audience.

"He was right. It reminded me of the movie *Desert Victory*, which was about Montgomery's attack on the Afrika Korps at

Alamein. We saw the Second Armored tanks move out at about 8 A.M. They took right off across the fields toward a wooded ridge line to the south, where we could see the German tanks milling about. The Second Armored tanks opened up all at once, and then the artillery behind them, and then P-47's and P-51's began to dive-bomb the ridge line.

"The noise was like the end of the world. The German tanks disappeared in the smoke, and all we could see was their muzzle flashes. Then there were a lot of big explosions on the ridge—I guess we had hit their ammunition dumps—and the whole damn woods disappeared in the smoke. The Krauts were still firing, though. Every once in a while I'd see an American tank get hit and go up in flames, with the guys scrambling out of it, their clothes on fire.

"By eleven o'clock it was all over. The last of the Second Armored tanks disappeared over the ridge and we didn't hear much firing after that. We must have beaten the shit out of that Second Panzer."

Actually, this was the typical worm's-eye view of battle experienced by most soldiers; and today, Grayson is the first to admit it. What he witnessed was only the opening skirmish in the battle. The rest of it was scattered over dozens of square miles and lasted for three days. While only one task force of Combat Command B of the Second Armored was attacking through Achene, a second task force was hitting the Celles pocket from Conneux and Conjeux, further south. The British 29th Armoured Brigade and the U.S. 82nd Reconnaissance Battalion were striking from the north toward the village of Foy Notre-Dame. Combat Command A, in the meantime, was fighting to the east and the south, near Rochefort, to prevent Panzer Lehr and the Ninth Panzer Division from breaking through to reinforce the Second Panzer at Celles. At least a hundred fighter-bombers from the U.S. Ninth Air Force also were involved in the desperate effort to prevent this link-up.

It wasn't until the morning of December 28 that the Second

Armored Division's General Ernest Harmon could report to First Army Headquarters that the trapped and crippled Second Panzer finally was wiped out. He listed the spoils of war: 88 German tanks, 75 heavy guns, 405 vehicles, 1,200 German prisoners, 2,500 German dead and wounded. "A great slaughter," General Harmon wearily concluded in his dispatch, which I saw later in official Pentagon postwar histories.

On that Christmas morning, the first day of the attack, all I saw were the American casualties—streaming back through the town in ambulances and sometimes on stretchers lashed to the hoods of jeeps.

I was smoking a cigarette outside the church when one such jeep stopped directly in front of me. The passenger on the hood was a youngster of about nineteen. His right thigh was shattered from knee to hip. He was still in shock and heavily dosed with morphine, but he asked me for a cigarette and I gave it to him. We talked briefly about what had happened to him.

He was an artilleryman. He had been so interested in the battle unfolding before him that he forgot to jump back after slamming a shell into the breech of his 105 howitzer. As the big gun fired the shell, its massive recoil caught him full on the leg—like a giant catapult.

I asked the boy how much combat time he had had in the war.

"Ten minutes," he said.

At about 4 P.M., Miller and Marcus, as was their habit, showed up from God knows where.

Marcus said, "The traffic pattern on the roads is reversed now. Most of it is medics, and they're heading north and west. I think we can get through to Dinant."

I went into the church to prepare the children for our rendezvous with the Red Cross, or whatever, in Dinant.

23

But when we got there, I just couldn't face it—not that day, anyway.

The ten-mile trip from Achene had been interminable. Time after time, MP's had waved us to the side of the road to let military convoys get through. When we did move, it was at a bumper-to-bumper pace. We didn't reach the outskirts of the city until long after dark. I had wanted the children to see Dinant's magnificent medieval citadel, perched high on a cliff over the Meuse River, and the beautiful onion-domed church nestled on the river bank just below it—but we could see nothing of the city's charm in the strictly imposed blackout.

The streets were clogged with civilian refugees from the countryside and with rear echelon troops of the British 29th Armoured Brigade. After we milled about in the dark for a while, it was Marcus who suggested that we spend the night in Dinant and look for the refugee center in the morning. I heaved a sigh of relief. At least I wouldn't have to give up the children in the cruel confusion of the night.

Miller said, "Let's find the limey command post and ask for a billet."

I had a better idea. I remembered that my pockets were crammed with Belgian francs, converted from the British pounds I had received for doing an illicit magazine piece for a

London publication. "Just across the river," I said, "is one of the finest ancient inns in Europe—the Auberge de Bouvignes. Let's spend the night there and come back to Dinant in the morning. We can get a good meal and a decent night's sleep. I pay."

Miller and Marcus looked at me peculiarly, I thought, but they agreed.

We crossed the sturdy stone bridge the Germans had wanted so desperately to cross and turned right, up the west bank of the river. After about two miles we came to the inn, nestled under a cliff beneath an eleventh-century fortification. The inn is built of hand-cut stone, covered over with pink stucco. It's leaded windows, like those in old churches, are set deep in the two-foot-thick walls. It has only six bedrooms but its gourmet restaurant has always been one of the best in Belgium.

For centuries the inn had been managed by people who served the noble Crèvecoeurs of the chateau on the cliff above. In 1944, the owners were a pleasant middle-aged couple who may or may not have been descendants of Crèvecoeurs serfs. They knew me from previous visits, and the innkeeper-chef, after a quick appraisal of Miller and Marcus and the children, informed me that though a British general and his aides were occupying four of his rooms, two were still available.

Also, though it was late, he rushed off to cook us a magnificent meal of Ardennes ham and fresh-caught trout, followed by a chocolate mousse for dessert. A bottle of 1937 Pouilly Fuissé was on the house. Miller and Marcus seemed uncomfortable in the rustic splendor of the inn's restaurant. The children were overwhelmed by it.

After dinner, drowsy from the unaccustomed richness of the meal after all those Army rations, we went upstairs to our rooms. Miller and Marcus shared one room; the children and I the other, larger one. It had two high beds covered with luxurious silken quilts. The rest of the furniture was rough-hewn and medieval-looking, and there was a tapestried rug on the floor. The children obviously had never seen anything like this in their lives.

We all took hot baths in the wonderfully deep European-style tub, and I rinsed out Lisa's nylons in the bathroom sink. I also hung out Freddie's still-damp hand-sewn underpants to dry. I wanted to talk with the children that night about the ordeal we were to face at the refugee center in the morning, but by the time I finished the chores in the bathroom, both Lisa and Freddie had flaked out on top of one of the beds. The room was chilly, and out of habit they had put on their overcoats over their naked bodies in preparation for sleep.

As gently as I could, I removed the overcoats and dressed each of them in a GI winter underwear top from my pack. The bottoms of the heavy flannel undershirts came to their ankles, like nightgowns, and I had to roll up the sleeves. They were only half awake as I tucked them into the bed under the quilt.

The two dark little heads seemed strange to me as they lay side by side on the clean white pillow, and I suddenly realized that this was the first time I ever had seen their hair. Until now, they had always kept on those pointy knit caps. Both had fine deep-brown hair, slightly copper-tinted. Lisa's was cut in a little girl's Dutch bob, with bangs across the forehead, and hung straight down over her ears. Somehow, while I was busy in the bathroom, she had managed to comb it. Freddie's hair was still rumpled from the cap.

I kissed them each on the cheek without waking them up and got into the other bed. I listened for a long time to the military traffic on both sides of the river, but eventually I fell asleep.

The children were up at 7 A.M., excitedly watching the boats and barges on the river through the leaded glass window. Then they insisted on taking batns again.

At eight o'clock there was a tap on the door, and the inn-keeper's wife came in with a breakfast tray. She had Ardennes ham and fried eggs and coffee for me, and soft-boiled eggs, croissants, and milk for the children. She clucked and fussed over Lisa and Freddie while they ate and rushed off with their shoes to scrape the mud off them. When she returned, she also had a bright red hair ribbon for Lisa.

After she left I watched the children get dressed, as if it were just another day. I had to help Lisa tuck her precious nylons in under the good black woolen stockings so that too many bumps wouldn't show. Freddie proudly showed me that his rash was better. It was, but not much. All the while, I kept struggling for the words to tell them that this was the day I'd have to leave them.

It was Lisa who solved the problem for me by bringing up the subject herself.

I won't attempt to record how the subsequent conversation went in our mongrelized mixture of English, French, and German, but this is how it turned out in my notes, in English:

LISA: Why can't we stay with you, papa?

ME: Because I'm a soldier, *Liebchen,* and soldiers can't have children with them while a war is still being fought. Besides, you really shouldn't call me papa.

FREDDIE: Why not, papa?

ME: Because I'm not really your papa. Once you had a papa of your own, and today I'm taking you to some people who will see to it that soon you will have another real papa—and a mama, too.

LISA: Why can't you marry Giselle and be our real papa?

ME: How did you know about Giselle?

FREDDIE: Sometimes you talk in your sleep, papa.

ME: Oh. Well. But that would not work out either, *Liebchens.* Giselle is not interested in marrying me. Besides, as I told you, soldiers are not permitted to have children with them.

LISA: But you have had us, since Spa.

ME: But that was different. There was no one else to help you.

LISA: But what if—in this place where you are taking us—there is no one to help us?

ME: But there will be, *Liebchen.* It is their duty. They will find a relative, an uncle perhaps, and you will go to live with him and you will have cousins to play with, like Gerhardt. Do you remember what fun it was to play with Gerhardt?

FREDDIE: Gerhardt's horse only has one eye.

ME: Yes, but it was fun playing with the horse, even with one eye, just the same, wasn't it?

FREDDIE: Yes, I guess so.

ME: So will you remember, when I take you to that place to-day, that soon you will have a real papa and cousins like Gerhardt to play with?

FREDDIE: Yes, papa.

LISA: Yes, papa.

ME: O.K., then?

LISA: No. I fear for you.

ME: What do you mean you fear for *me?*

LISA: You will continue your journey with the two men, the two sergeants?

ME: Yes, why?

LISA: Freddie and I do not like them.

ME: Like them? Why not?

LISA: They speak German.

ME: Why that's ridiculous, Lisa. The soldier in the farmhouse spoke German. Many American soldiers speak German. It is part of their duty.

FREDDIE: But none speak German the way the two sergeants do.

ME: Forget it, *Liebchen.* The two sergeants only speak German so well because they were taught to do so for a radio station in which all speak German.

FREDDIE: All right. But Lisa and I still do not like the two sergeants.

ME: Well, that is not important. What is important is that when I take you into that place today, I want you to be brave and understanding so that I will be proud of you. You do want me to be proud of you, don't you?

LISA: Bet your ass, papa.

24

Dinant by daylight was even more chaotic than it had been the night before. Refugees still were streaming in from the east, evacuees from the fighting around Celles and beyond. Many were passing over the Bouvignes bridge to safer, more distant havens; but hundreds of others swarmed aimlessly around the streets of the city. Because of the frightened, frustrated crowds of strangers, most of the merchants had shuttered their shops. They dealt mostly in the exquisite hand-hammered copper household items, which Dinant's unique craftsmen had fashioned for centuries. At the time, there wasn't much demand for this sort of luxury merchandise.

I crossed the bridge in the jeep, with the children. Miller and Marcus had remained behind to wait for me at the inn.

I didn't have much trouble finding the refugee center after parking the jeep along the river bank near the bridge. I simply followed the crowds. The refugee center was an impromptu affair set up on an emergency basis on the ground floor of one of the public buildings near the church and the street of copperware shops. It was teeming with people, many of them stretched out on the floor.

At the far end of the room were several glassed-in offices. In front of each stood a long line of patient refugees. Behind a table in one of the offices, I saw an elderly woman wearing some sort of bluish uniform. The uniform didn't have the familiar Red Cross shoulder patch but there was a makeshift armband, with an inked red cross, around the woman's right arm. I got into that line, the children clinging to me.

The refugees stared at my uniform and at the children, then politely waved me up to the head of the line. In less than ten minutes I was in the office, facing the woman in blue. The rest of her was gray—gray hair, gray face. She was in her sixties, with an indeterminate figure, and she looked exhausted. I guessed that she had been up most of the night.

I told her my story in French, since she made it clear at once that she "did not have English." Her own French was cosmopolitan and could have been French, Belgian, or Swiss. When she had finished listening to my rambling account, she said, "All right, monsieur, we will accept the children. They are Jews, you say? That is good. There are excellent Jewish refugee organizations, well financed and well organized."

It all seemed a little cold-blooded to me, and I got pissed off. The woman looked kind enough, and in fairness to her, I suppose she had seen so many homeless children that two more were just that.

But goddamit, these were *my* kids. My smart, brave, laughing, crying, hurt, trusting kids. I started to tell the woman about the rash on Freddie's crotch, but she cut me short with, "Never mind, monsieur. These children will be given a thorough examination. They will be hospitalized, if necessary. They will be properly cared for." She got painfully to her feet and came around to my side of the table.

"But they *are* properly cared for," I bellowed.

A look of astonishment crossed the woman's face, and she grasped each child by the hand—not roughly, not gently. She simply stood there, holding Lisa's right hand and Freddie's left hand, staring at me.

A knot of people gathered outside the office, peering in to see what the shouting was all about. I lowered my voice and said, "What I mean is, my, these children have been properly cared for. And I don't think Freddie would like being in a hospital, at least not unless you let Lisa stay with him. And Lisa's to keep the nylon drawers I made for her because she . . ."

The woman's look of astonishment increased. She glanced quickly at the region around Lisa's non-existent hips, then back at my face—which I'm sure by then was apoplectic—and back to Lisa again. All through my outburst, Freddie had never taken his eyes off me. Neither had Lisa. They just stood there quietly, their hands captive in the woman's hands, their faces closed and still, the way I first had seen them in Spa.

Suddenly the woman released her hold on them. She cleared her throat, smiled as if at last she understood, and said, "Monsieur, you'll want to say goodbye." She turned quickly and slumped out of the office, leaving Lisa, Freddie, and me standing alone in the barren room.

The children looked so little then. So young. So ancient. So sad. I sank to a squatting position in front of them. Their four brown eyes were level with my two brown eyes. But theirs, as my vision blurred, began to run together like four bits of melting chocolate.

"*Mein Kinder,*" I began. But I couldn't seem to think of anything else to say. Because four small hands were holding my head against first one skinny chest then the other, and two hearts were beating hard and fast against my forehead.

And then they were gone.

25

I was late getting back to the inn because I stopped off at the Hôtel des Postes for a half-liter of wine which I drank quickly at a spotted zinc table in the crowded dining room. And then it took a long time to get through the tangle of refugees, horse-drawn vehicles and bicycles crossing the bridge at Bouvignes.

As I pulled up in front of the inn, Miller and Marcus were waiting outside. They had packed my things as well as theirs. "Let's haul ass," said Marcus. "It's late. We've got to get to Paris." Not one word about the children.

I blew up. "If you're in such a fucking hurry to get to Paris, why don't you get your own fucking jeep?"

Marcus' eyes hardened, but Miller said, "Calm down. Since your outfit hasn't heard from you in ten days, I expect you'd better worry about getting to Paris in a hurry."

That stopped me. The *Yank* bureau hadn't been in contact with me for more than ten days. Probably figured I was dead by now, or AWOL. I'd better check in. "How about the telephone?"

"No chance," Miller said. "We already tried that. Nothing but priority headquarters calls can get through."

I went inside to pay the bill, and we took off for Paris.

At the bridge across the river to Dinant, we turned right

on a road that was marked "À *Reims, France.*" Less than a mile from the river, except for occasional military vehicles and clusters of refugees, most of the signs of the war had receded.

I was driving and Miller was beside me in the children's seat. Marcus was in the back. They were totally uncommunicative now. I stole a glance at them and noticed that both had unslung their carbines. The weapons were resting lightly across their knees.

I was only subliminally aware of that at the time. Carbines, though smaller than rifles, are, after all, uncomfortable when you're seated and they're strapped to your shoulder. On the Reims road out of Dinant, I simply wondered where they had kept the carbines before. I figured they must have been in the back in the *Lootwagen.*

My mind was almost totally on the children as I drove. What would they be doing now? Was a doctor examining them? Was some officious bitch trying to take Lisa's nylons away from her? Were they lonely and frightened? I consoled myself with the thought that they probably were with other children by now—the security of being with kids in the same predicament would tend to neutralize the anxiety. But then I began to worry about whether the other children would tease them because of their speech. There wouldn't be any German kids there, and how many people spoke pidgin French-English-German? I calmed down when I remembered the Belgian German-speaking minority from the Eupen-Malmédy border area. Certainly some children from there must have reached Dinant, too. Also, I reminded myself, the Luxembourgeois speak a bastardized form of German.

The language problem made me think of the conversation I had had with Lisa and Freddie in our room at the inn the night before. Why didn't they like Marcus and Miller? It couldn't be just because the two sergeants spoke flawless German. Or could it? Marcus and Miller had said they'd learned German because they were in the security detachment for the

German-speaking Psychological Warfare soldiers at Radio Luxembourg. Would such German taught to them at Cornell University be flawless? I had had four years of French at NYU, and my accent and grammatical errors caused tolerant smiles on the part of any French or Belgian I talked to.

I began to sweat as I reviewed in my mind the circumstances of my relationship with Marcus and Miller.

They had been alone in the *Forêt de Freyr* when the children and I came upon them. They said they had been commandeered by an American general and forced to fight at St. Vith. If that was true, why hadn't they fallen back with the other American troops to the secondary defense line they said was still in being to the west of St. Vith? Why had they continued on alone, past Bastogne?

Then there was that peculiar radio they carried. They'd seemed nervous when I asked them if it was a walkie-talkie. And how had they been able to use it to pinpoint the locations of the German units so exactly? They would have had to have understood the slang and the code names. How could they have known, just from the radio, that the German General Bayerlein's nickname was "Iron-ass?" Would the German troops of the elite Panzer Lehr Division have dared to have used such a disparaging allusion to their commanding general over the open airwaves? With, possibly, the Gestapo listening in?

Marcus and Miller had said it was their reference to Iron-ass that got us across the Rochefort bridge. But that passage through the German lines, wasn't it *too* easy? Where had they really got those Kraut camouflage suits? What had they really said to the Kraut MP's at the Rochefort bridge? Had the children heard something they were afraid to tell me about?

And then, Dinant. Why had Marcus and Miller persisted in hanging around waiting for me and my jeep? Surely they could have gone to the British command post and gotten their own ride to Paris. There must be vehicles going back and forth all the time.

Paris.

I thought of the carbines in Marcus' and Miller's laps. What better way for Skorzeny's SS commandos to get through to Paris than with a schmuck American correspondent?

I had to think.

There were roadblocks, Ray had said. All over France, Belgium, and the Netherlands. Roadblocks where the CIC (Counterintelligence Corps) asked trick questions to try and trap the Skorzeny men. Questions like, "What's the capital of Missouri? Are the Chicago Cubs in the National or the American League?"

Roadblocks. We had to be getting to one soon. But what good would that do? If I gave Marcus and Miller away, they'd just shoot me first and risk getting killed themselves. That's the way SS men were. They didn't give a shit—if they got caught in American uniforms, they'd be executed as spies anyway.

No, I'd have to think of something more subtle at the first roadblock.

But where was it?

It was at Hastière, about ten kilometers from Dinant, and it couldn't have been in a more perfect place for its specialized purposes. I could see the roadblock from quite some distance away as I coasted down a long slope along the Meuse River bank.

Just before it entered the village, the road passed through a defile, one side of which was a craggy stone cliff. On the other side was one of those high stone walls you see everywhere in the outskirts of Belgian villages. Between the wall and the cliff, two Army command cars had been parked, parallel, in the middle of the road. With the natural and artificial stone obstructions on either side, the only way to pass the two command cars was to zigzag between them. I could see about a dozen GI's lounging around the command cars. Some of them wore MP armbands. Others were in plain uniforms with not even insignia of rank. These, I knew, were the CIC agents.

By now, I knew what I was going to do.

I slowed down. Marcus, seeing the roadblock, growled something at Miller. I pulled up to the first command car and stopped just in front of an MP holding up his hand.

One of the CIC men came over and strolled around the jeep, peering in at us. He had a holster at his waist, and I could see the butt of a .45 protruding from it. The top of the holster was unbuttoned. The MP's also wore .45's, but some of them carried M-1 rifles as well.

The CIC man came over to my side of the jeep. "Where were you born, sir?" he asked.

"New Jersey."

"Where in New Jersey?"

"Jersey City."

"Would you mind telling me what's the capital of New Jersey?"

I gulped and blurted out, *"Newark!"*

Then, without waiting for a reaction, I grabbed the steering wheel with both hands and propelled myself sideways out of the jeep, falling heavily to the road on my left shoulder and upper arm.

I was stunned for a minute or two, but I heard a lot of scuffling and yelling.

Then, two shots.

I had brushed the CIC man's legs on my way down and could see his boots for an instant.

But then I couldn't see them or anything else anymore.

26

I was taken to a room somewhere. It was the living room of a prosperous-looking civilian house, and a CIC captain was sitting on a couch behind a coffee table and drinking tea from a delicate blue-and-white Delft cup. The captain was big and pudgy, with bulging brown eyes and only a few strands of black hair plastered across the top of his balding head.

He told me to sit down in the chair opposite him. His accent was New York City. He looked Jewish, but he could have been Italian, Greek, or Armenian. I guessed he was about thirty, younger than he seemed.

The captain studied me while he finished drinking his tea. He didn't offer me any, but if he had, I was probably still too shaken to hold even the flimsy cup.

He asked me for my correspondent's credentials and I passed him the little SHAEF folder which, in addition to my photograph and signature, also featured a beautiful set of my fingerprints. The captain looked at the ID, nodded, handed it back to me.

"You went to NYU, didn't you?"

Astonished at the question, I said, "Yes. Why?"

"I used to watch you in the track meets in Madison Square Garden," he observed. "The way you ran the hurdles, you must have a lot of splinters in your balls."

I grunted. "What has that got to do with what happened at the roadblock?"

"I was coming to that." The captain poured himself another cup of tea. "Suppose you give me your version first."

"Version? What version?" I said. "You know what happened as well as I do. I came to the roadblock. I said Newark instead of Trenton for the capital of New Jersey. I fell out of the jeep. There was a fight. And your men got the Krauts, I guess." Then, suddenly worried, I added, "They did get the Krauts, didn't they?"

The captain sipped his tea. "Before I answer that question, let me give you my version."

"I don't understand all this crap about versions. What happened, happened. How many versions can there be?"

"All right," the captain said politely. "I'll put it another way. Let me acquaint you with the facts as I understand them, prior to the time you were brought in here."

"That's better," I said.

"All right," the captain said. He stretched out a heavy leg on the coffee table. "At about eleven o'clock this morning, I got a phone call from British MI5 in Dinant. That's British Army Intelligence, you understand."

I nodded and he went on. "The major there, whom I know, told me a wild story. He said that some joker in a correspondent's uniform had turned over two German Jewish refugee kids to the civilian evacuee center there. The correspondent left and then the children began crying and screaming and kicking up a storm. They said they wanted to talk to a soldier. No one could understand these kids very well because they spoke a mixture of French, English, and German, so they sent for a German-speaking MI5 lieutenant. The kids told the lieutenant that the correspondent was traveling west, to Paris probably, and that there were two Germans wearing American uniforms in his jeep. The children were so agitated that the lieutenant believed them."

I felt a surge of pride and affection for my kids. "How about that!"

He ignored my interruption and continued. "As you undoubtedly know, Otto Skorzeny's commandos are loose in the countryside, so naturally this information interested us. Since we have six roadblocks set up on all the roads leading out of Dinant, we awaited your arrival. We thought you would long since have passed the one at Hastière. But that's where you showed up. The rest of my version of what happened coincides with yours."

I smiled happily.

"Except for one thing," he muttered through a mouthful of tea.

"What's that?"

"Schmuck!" he said. "Those weren't Krauts in your jeep, they were two of my men!"

I sagged. "Your men?"

"Yes. Counterintelligence Corps, United States Army. They had come all the way back from the other side of the Losheim Gap, only to run into this."

"You mean Marcus and Miller?"

"Is that what they were calling themselves?" The captain had regained his composure. "Yes, we use those names a lot."

"But what happened to them at the roadblock?"

"One of them got shot in the ass."

"Who? Marcus or Miller?"

"How do I know? I never could tell those two apart."

I sat there, stunned, while the captain drank some more tea. Then, in a weak voice I asked, "What about me? Can I go now?"

He shrugged. "Why not? I can't arrest a man for falling out of a jeep."

I struggled to my feet and walked to the door. Before I got there I said, "Just one thing puzzles me. Why didn't Marcus and Miller get their own vehicle in Dinant instead of waiting to go on with me?"

"I'll never be able to figure it out, but they liked you. They said you were such a schmuck out in the field that they wanted to stick with you to keep you from getting yourself hurt."

Total deflation. "The wound in the ass, was it serious?"

"Not bad. He'll be out of the hospital in a couple, three days."

Before I opened the door to leave, I said meekly, "You've been very nice about this. Would you mind telling me your name, sir?"

"Not at all," he said. "Miller. Captain Marcus Miller."

27

I crossed the border to Givet, in France, where I drowned my embarrassment in Pouilly Fuissé—and tried to figure out how I was going to face *another* Miller. Merle Miller, that is, who later would become a distinguished novelist, critic, and commentator on homosexuality. At that time, Merle was the *Yank* correspondent in charge of the Paris Bureau of the magazine, and, in editorial matters, my superior. A Master Sergeant, he was the only *Yank* man in the theater who persisted in wearing his stripes on his uniform.

I had thought of asking tne CIC captain to teletype Merle, advising him of my survival. But knowing my bureau chief, I figured he might then request more information as to why the CIC was furnishing information about me—an eventuality that could lead to worldwide dissemination of the details of my humiliation. I decided it would be more appropriate for me to drop into the Paris office unannounced, give Miller the outline of my experiences with the children (leaving out the roadblock incident completely), and then sit out as much as possible of the rest of the Battle of the Bulge writing the story right there in Paris.

I didn't get along very well with Merle. He was an agrarian intellectual from Iowa, and I gravitated more to big-city boys like myself or Saul Levitt, a wise and irreverent Bronx sage whose subsequent works included the hit play, *The Andersonville Trial.*

Merle had more than proved his writing ability and his bravery when he covered several bitter campaigns for *Yank* in the South Pacific, before being transferred to the desk job in Paris. In fact, he was side by side with one of our photographers, John Bushemi, in the landing on Eniwetok, when Bushemi was killed. Miller was saved when a shell fragment glanced off a Bible, printed in the primitive Marshallese language, which he had been carrying in his blouse pocket. We heard that the Army had sent him to lecture on this phenomenon in some of the more God-fearing sections of the United States. Then he had been sent to us.

Perhaps it was because he had been conditioned to the more stringent operating procedures that General Douglas MacArthur imposed on *Yank* in his Pacific Theater, but Merle never really cottoned to our Eisenhower-encouraged freewheeling ways in Europe.

For example, he couldn't understand why I should have my own room at the Scribe Hotel, the press headquarters in Paris, when I came back from the combat zone. I tried to explain to Merle that this was because of my friendship with Major Charles Madary, who ran the hotel for the Army; but Merle, who slept in an Army billet, commandeered my room after sending me off on my assignment with the *maquis*. He told Major Madary that it was a *Yank* room, not a Davidson room, and that since he outranked me he was taking it over. Madary, of course, threw him out. The Major suggested to me that in order to avoid embarrassment in the future, I should always register at the Scribe under a different name—*any* name. So I came up with identities such as George Armstrong Custer of *The Sioux Nations Tomahawk* and Faisal P. Mohammed of the Jersey City (N.J.) *Jewish Standard*.

This time, when I arrived at the Scribe late in the evening of December 26, I registered as Josip Broz of the Newtown

194

(Conn.) *Bee.* I got my old room back, took a bath, and—because I couldn't stop thinking about Freddie and Lisa—tried to put a call through to Dinant. "Sorry, Mac," said the Army telephone operator. "All the civilian circuits have been taken over by SHAEF." He didn't know it and I didn't know it, but Supreme Headquarters knew it: The final battle to relieve the siege of Bastogne was just about to get under way.

I went downstairs, had a cold dinner, and wandered into the hotel bar, which even at this late hour was usually jammed with civilian correspondents. The bar was nearly empty. Most of the correspondents were at the front or at the various Army Group and Army headquarters, where communications were better and closer to the source of news.

I had a couple of cognacs with Major Madary, but then he left, and I got so bored that I even went to a late SHAEF briefing. Only a few French and British reporters were there. The briefing officer droned on about events I knew were at least two days old. He didn't even mention that the Second Armored had attacked the Second Panzer at Celles.

When it was over, I went back to the bar and shared a bottle of white wine with one of the French journalists. We had a totally unconstructive argument about the greatness or lack of greatness of De Gaulle. Then I dragged myself off to my room and went to bed.

I slept until noon.

When I got up, after lounging in bed in pajamas for the first time in weeks, I felt considerably better. I breakfasted and tried to call Dinant again, with the same result. I got dressed and decided I'd better get over to the office.

The *Yank* Bureau was on the second floor of the Shell Building, just down the street from the Paris *Herald-Tribune* on the Rue de Berri, near the Champs-Elysées. When I walked in the writers' bullpen was empty, save for Martine, our French stenographer. I attempted to pinch Martine's exquisite bottom, my usual greeting, but she said *"Non, non,"* and flashed a diamond ring at me. She had become engaged to an Australian consular attaché since I'd last left for the front.

I congratulated her, rather sourly, and asked who was in the office.

"Just the art department and Monsieur Miller."

I sauntered over to Merle's desk. His brown eyes regarded me suspiciously through his owl-like eyeglasses. "It's about time we heard from you. What have you got? New York needs copy about the big German offensive."

I started to detail the story of my strange odyssey with Freddie and Lisa.

"What kind of story is that?" he interrupted me. "Go back to Luxembourg and get us some real combat stuff about the war!"

Epilogue

Everyone who has heard this story asks me the same question: Did I ever see or hear from Lisa and Freddie again?

The answer is no.

I returned to Luxembourg and knocked out a few mediocre pieces for *Yank* while the Allies counterattacked and pushed the Germans back across the Siegfried Line and to the Rhine. My heart just wasn't in it anymore. By the time I could get through to Dinant on the phone, the temporary refugee center had been disassembled and its personnel and records transferred elsewhere.

In January—probably after evaluating the quality of my writing and noting that my carelessness nearly resulted in my being killed by a sniper near Esch—205 East 42nd Street decided that my seven months in the combat zone were enough and I was ordered home. I got my Troop Carrier Command friends to fly me directly to England and conned myself into a ride across the Atlantic in a U.S. Navy destroyer escort. I slept in the Captain's sea-cabin next to the bridge—until he found out I was an Army enlisted man and not a civilian. The Navy's sense of rank being what it is, I was treated with pissed off coolness for the last two days of the trip and deposited on a dock in Brooklyn without so much as a goodbye.

I hung around the New York headquarters of *Yank*, doing

sports columns and such for a while. When the war in Europe ended, someone added up my inflated but impressive number of points for combat time and decorations, and I found myself in the first group of GI's sent to the Fort Dix Demobilization Center for discharge from the Army.

As soon as I had shed the military, I went to work for *Collier's* as an Associate Editor. I got caught up in the swinging life of a writer for a then prestigious magazine, in New York, Washington, and Hollywood, pretty much returning to my old self-serving ways.

It wasn't until I married in 1947 and began to consider having children that I became plagued again by the memory of Lisa and Freddie. I wrote to the Red Cross and to all the refugee organizations I could think of in Paris and Brussels, but the answers all were the same. They were polite, but sorry. There were so many children, and since I could not furnish them with a correct last name, and since some of the Dinant records had been destroyed on their way to Brussels as the result of enemy air action . . .

In 1953, when I was in Europe on an assignment for *Collier's,* I enlisted the aid of a friend of mine in the Joint Distribution Committee, a powerful international Jewish organization with contacts in all the refugee groups. He finally came up with a list of pairs of children who matched my specifications of Lisa and Freddie. One pair had been sent to relatives in São Paulo, Brazil, earlier refugees from Hitler's Germany. Another pair had gone to an uncle in Rumania, still another to cousins in Poland. A fourth set of children had died of typhoid in an internment camp on Cyprus while they were on their way to Israel. My friend hastened to assure me that from the descriptions he had received from the British Army, he was pretty certain that the Cyprus children were not mine.

I ran up against a blank wall in Rumania and Poland, the Iron Curtain countries, but I did get a response from the people in Brazil, who sent photographs. The children were blond and blue-eyed.

When the Cold War thawed, I tried Rumania and Poland again—but with no success.

Finally, last year, I went back to Spa to look for the woman who had turned Lisa and Freddie over to me in the first place, hoping I could pick up the trail from her and follow it back through her sister in Germany.

The Hôtel du Portugal, outside of which the woman had stood with the children, was still there. But it now is mostly a coffee shop for the young fans who attend the rock concerts at the casino across the square. My nameless woman was totally unknown to the current residents. The grand old hotels and resorts have been taken over by entrepreneurs from Brussels and Antwerp. In fact, the town now is more of a weekend vacation center for swingers than the staid watering place for the elderly it had been when its hot-springs baths were world-famous.

The entire Ardennes has changed. There are TV antennae on the thousand-year-old farmhouses, and the native young dress in the manner of *Mod Squad*. There are American-style supermarkets at the crossroads, and the Ardennais now swarm about in Volkswagens and Simcas instead of on bicycles. The great fir forests are dotted with resort inns ("Catch your own trout in our private stream and our chef will prepare it for you") and camping sites, and even golf courses. The primitive woods and lush farms are still there, but on the whole, the region reminded me of the Catskills. The Monticello of these Catskills is La Roche. On the bluffs above the Ourthe River, for which we so bitterly contested the Germans, are hotels— one after the other—with names like *Air Pur* and *Belle-Vue*.

There is no sign of war, except for the highly profitable "Nuts Museum" in Bastogne, and the beautifully simple memorial at the site of the Malmédy Massacre: the Baugnez crossroads. The memorial is a shrine and a stone wall with the names of the victims set into it in metallic plaques. It saddened me to see the name of "P. Davidson," the young boy in the 285th Artillery Observation Battalion with whom I had joked about the possibility of our being related.

There was no clue to Lisa and Freddie. Just the painfully reawakened memory.

I now have my own daughter, Carol. I think of her in terms of being a few years younger than Lisa and Freddie, who today would be in their early thirties.

To me, however, they still are six and seven.

Perhaps I prefer it that way.